the Micheff Sisters
Cooking
with

Kellogg's ®

To Rose,
may all your meals be
seasoned with God's Love!

Linda A. Sasser ☺

Also by the Micheff sisters
Cooking With the Micheff Sisters
Cooking Entrées With the Micheff Sisters
Cooking for Two With the Micheff Sisters
Soups, Salads & Sandwiches With the Micheff Sisters
Family Favorites With the Micheff Sisters

Cover recipe: Tamale Vegetable Casserole, p. 120

Designer: Chrystique Neibauer
Portrait photos: Chrystique Neibauer
Recipe photos: Mark Mosrie
Copyeditor: Mellisa Hoffman
Project Manager: Mellisa Hoffman

Additional copies of this book can be purchased at 3ABN:
Call 618-627-4651 or visit online at www.3abn.org
Adventist Book Centers®: Call toll-free 1-800-765-6955 or visit online at
www.adventistbookcenter.com.

ISBN 13: 978-0-8163-5206-7 (pbk.)
ISBN 10: 0-8163-5206-2 (pbk.)

February 2014

the Micheff Sisters
Cooking with *Kellogg's*®

A Vegan Vegetarian Cookbook

Pacific Press®
Publishing Association

Nampa, Idaho | Oshawa, Ontario, Canada
www.pacificpress.com

Foreword

For over 100 years the Kellogg Company has supported the benefits of a vegetarian diet and lifestyle. It's a history that began with Dr. John Harvey Kellogg, who developed good health and dietary practices to achieve holistic well-being. In celebration of these healthful efforts, Kellogg is delighted to recommend this cookbook to vegetarians, as well as to anyone who appreciates a really good meal.

You'll find that these vegetarian dishes will impress hungry appetites and expand your culinary range. They are flavorful, tempting recipes that include meat alternative products like Worthington® and Loma Linda®, MorningStar Farms®, and Gardenburger®, which bring a variety of tastes to the dinner table so everyone is happy.

So put your apron on, grab some pans, and explore the deliciously exciting possibilities of vegetarian cuisine. We hope you enjoy sharing these recipes with your family and friends as much as we enjoy sharing them with you.

Eat in good health!

Barry Shepard
Vice President, Marketing and Innovation
Kellogg US Frozen Foods

Table of Contents

Introduction

When we were little, our parents made the decision to stop eating meat and switch to a healthier diet. For protein they added nuts, grains, and legumes, and balanced it out with fresh fruits and vegetables. Mom also added some tasty meat alternatives to enhance our meals.

We grew up loving many of the products from **Loma Linda**® and **Worthington**®, such as their Big Franks, **Linketts**™, **Vege-Burger**®, **Vegetable Skallops**®, and so many of their other meat substitutes. We really didn't miss the meat because we enjoyed the vegetarian meat-like products so much. Mom learned to fix them in ways that even our meat-eating friends enjoyed—especially her vegeburgers! In our eyes, Mom was the best cook in the world and made the most mouth-watering, tastiest food ever! Today, thanks to Kellogg's, there are even more meatless products to choose from, so our children not only love the foods we grew up with, but have new favorites of their own from **MorningStar Farms**® and **Gardenburger**®!

Now that we are grown, we see the value in investing in God's health-care plan! When mad-cow disease hit the news, it seemed like everyone was afraid to eat meat and vegeburgers reached a new level of popularity. Amazingly, it has been proven that there are many health benefits from having a vegetarian diet and that having a meat-less diet even helps in reducing the risk of many diseases including cancer and cardio-vascular disease.

We are thankful that Kellogg's provides so many meatless products that are not only disease-free but delicious as well! God has provided so many wonderful things for us to enjoy and in Psalm 34:8, He invites us to "taste and see that He is good"! It is our prayer that this cookbook will be a blessing to all and another step closer to better health!

With God's richest blessings,

The Micheff Sisters

Linda, Brenda, and Cinda

Breakfast

Sunshine
Strudel p. 29

Sausage Biscuit
Rollups p. 23

Breakfast
Scramble p. 17

Florentine
Mushroom Quiche
p. 19

Baked Potato
Hash p. 12

Biscuit Burgers
p. 24

Baked Potato Hash

3 large potatoes

1 20-ounce can *Loma Linda* Big Franks

1 medium onion, coarsely chopped

1 cup red or yellow sweet pepper, coarsely chopped

1 teaspoon red pepper flakes

1 teaspoon salt

2 tablespoons McKay's Chicken Style Seasoning

½ cup jalapeño nacho slices (optional)

Bake potatoes until tender. Cool and coarsely chop.

Cut *Loma Linda* Big Franks into ¼ to ½ inch slices. Spray a skillet with nonstick cooking spray. Sauté *Loma Linda* Big Franks over medium-high heat until browned on both sides. Set aside.

Sauté onion in a skillet that has been sprayed with nonstick cooking spray over medium heat until clear. Add sweet peppers and red pepper flakes. Sauté until tender. Add potatoes, *Loma Linda* Big Franks, salt, McKay's Chicken Style Seasoning, and jalapeños. Sauté until potatoes are golden brown. Serve hot.

Sunday morning breakfast is a really big deal at my house, and it just wouldn't be the same without Baked Potato Hash. This recipe usually changes from week to week depending on what ingredients I have on hand. The idea started when I had some leftover baked potatoes I needed to use up, which, oddly enough, some of my best recipes start this way! But if you have boiled potatoes—that works too! —Brenda

Yield: 16 ½-cup servings

(½ cup) Calories 100 Total Fat 1.5g Saturated Fat 0g Sodium 450mg Total Carbohydrates 15g Fiber 3g Protein 8g

Hungry Man Hash

Heat a large skillet that has been sprayed with nonstick cooking spray over medium heat. Add onions and sauté until they are clear. Add potatoes, seasonings, and **Loma Linda® Linketts™**, then cover with a lid. Stir every five minutes until potatoes are soft and golden brown.

My family loves potatoes for any meal and fixed about any way I can think of! I love seeing the smiles on their faces when I prepare special favorites for them. I've added this potato dish to their list of favorites! You can also use it as a filling for a breakfast burrito. Just put the potato mixture into a whole-wheat tortilla and add avocado, vegan cheese, fresh tomatoes, Tofutti Better Than Sour Cream, and salsa. Serve with a colorful fruit salad. —Linda

1 cup onions, diced fine

3 cups raw potatoes, peeled and diced thin

½ teaspoon salt

½ teaspoon seasoned salt

½ teaspoon red pepper flakes

2 cups **Loma Linda® Linketts™**, sliced

Yield: 8 ½-cup servings

(½ cup) Calories 120 Total Fat 4g Saturated Fat 0.5g Sodium 440mg Total Carbohydrates 13g Fiber 3g Protein 9g

Sweet Potato Hash

1 tablespoon canola oil

1 cup onion, slivered

½ teaspoon salt

½ teaspoon seasoned salt

½ teaspoon red pepper flakes

1½ cup cooked sweet potatoes, cut in small slices

1 19-ounce can *Loma Linda* Little Links

2 cups cooked potatoes, diced

2 tablespoons chives for garnish, fresh or dried

In a large skillet on medium heat, place the canola oil, onions, seasonings, and sweet potatoes. Cover and sauté for approximately 5 to 10 minutes. Add the potatoes and **Loma Linda** Little Links and sauté until golden brown and onions are tender. Serve hot!

Little Links are one of my family favorites, and sweet potatoes make the links taste even better and add extra nutrition too! Whether served on a brunch buffet or just by themselves, they are sure to please!
—Linda

Yield: 10 ½-cup servings

(½ cup) Calories 150 Total Fat 6g Saturated Fat 1g Sodium 420mg Total Carbohydrates 15g Fiber 3g Protein 9g

German Potato Fry

In a large skillet that has been sprayed with nonstick cooking spray, sauté the onions over medium-high heat until they are clear. Add the celery, red and yellow peppers, salt, and seasoned salt. Continue sautéing until the vegetables are crunchy tender, then add the frozen potatoes and *Loma Linda* Big Franks and sauté until golden brown. Serve hot!

This German Potato Fry is colorful and delicious and can be served morning, noon, or evening. It is a dish that can be made the day before and warmed in a skillet the next morning. I love the one-dish meals that are not only nutritious but save me so much time! I like to serve this with homemade wheat toast and a fresh fruit salad.
—Linda

2 cups onions, chopped fine

1½ cups celery, thinly sliced

1 cup yellow peppers, julienne cut

1 cup red peppers, julienne cut

1 teaspoon seasoned salt

1 teaspoon salt

6 cups frozen shredded potatoes

1 20-ounce can *Loma Linda* Big Franks, sliced

Yield: 7 ½-cup servings

(½ cup) Calories 270 Total Fat 4g Saturated Fat 0.5g Sodium 1010mg Total Carbohydrates 41g Fiber 6g Protein 18g

Vegetable Potato Rosti

1 10-ounce package *Gardenburger Veggie Medley*® Veggie Burgers

4 cups potatoes, shredded

¼ cup onion, finely diced

2 tablespoons olive oil

Crumble **Gardenburger Veggie Medley**® Veggie Burgers and combine with potatoes and onions in a medium-sized bowl.

Add ½ tablespoon olive oil to an 8-inch nonstick skillet and heat to medium high. Evenly coat the bottom of the skillet with the oil. Add potato mixture to skillet and spread evenly to the sides. Cover and cook over medium heat. Add additional oil as needed. When browned on the bottom, slide onto a round pan or plate, add another ½ tablespoon of oil to the hot skillet and flip the rosti back on to the hot skillet, browned side up. Cover and cook until browned on other side.

I love potato hash for breakfast, lunch, or supper! Basically that's because I just love potatoes! This recipe was inspired by my grandma Micheff, who made the best fried potatoes ever! However, I wanted to add a bit of protein to the dish and came up with this recipe. The **Gardenburger Veggie Medley**® *Veggie Burgers have just the right seasonings, so you don't need to add any more. You'll not only love the flavor but the texture is great too. —Brenda*

Yield: 2 8-inch potato rostis

(¼ rosti) Calories 140 Total Fat 5g Saturated Fat 0.5g Sodium 190mg Total Carbohydrates 23g Fiber 4g Protein 3g

Breakfast Scramble

In a large skillet on medium-high heat, place the canola oil and onions and sauté for approximately 5 minutes. Add the **Worthington® Vegetable Skallops®,** potatoes, and salt and sauté until golden brown.

In a medium-sized bowl, mash the tofu, then add the remaining seasonings. Mix well and add to the skillet. Simmer for another 3 to 4 minutes. Serve hot.

I love making one-dish meals that my family enjoys. My husband likes to have potatoes at least once a day, and these mouth-watering **Worthington® Vegetable Skallops®** *make this recipe even better! Try this delicious* **Worthington® Vegetable Skallops®** *scrambled tofu dish rolled up in warm tortillas with salsa, avocado, tomatoes, Tofutti Better Than Sour Cream, and salsa! —Linda*

- 1 cup onions, diced
- 1 tablespoon canola oil
- 2 cups **Worthington® Vegetable Skallops®**, diced fine
- 1 cup potatoes, diced
- ½ teaspoon salt
- 1 12.4-ounce package extra-firm Mori-Nu Tofu
- ½ teaspoon McKay's Chicken Style Seasoning
- ¼ teaspoon turmeric
- 1 teaspoon nutritional yeast flakes
- ½ teaspoon seasoned salt

Yield: 7 ½-cup servings

(½ cup) Calories 130 Total Fat 3.5g Saturated Fat 0g Sodium 630mg Total Carbohydrates 9g Fiber 3g Protein 14g

Urban Omelet

Filling:
1 tablespoon canola oil
1 medium onion, diced
1½ cups baby portabella mushrooms, coarsely chopped
1 20-ounce can *Worthington Vegetable Skallops*, cut into thin strips
2 cups cooked potatoes, diced
1 tablespoon McKay's Chicken Style Seasoning
½ teaspoon red pepper flakes
2 teaspoons dried chervil or parsley

Omelet:
1 12-ounce package firm water-packed tofu, drained and pressed
1 tablespoon original soymilk or almond milk
1 tablespoon cornstarch
2½ tablespoons nutritional yeast flakes
1 teaspoon garlic powder
1 teaspoon Italian seasoning
½ teaspoon ground turmeric
1 teaspoon McKay's Chicken Style Seasoning
¼ teaspoon paprika

Lemon Pesto:
2 packed cups fresh spinach leaves
4 packed cups fresh basil leaves
4–5 tablespoons extra virgin olive oil
4 tablespoons fresh lemon juice
1 tablespoon lemon zest
¾ teaspoon salt
½ cup walnuts
1 clove fresh garlic
1 teaspoon nutritional yeast flakes
2 tablespoons water

For the Filling: Heat a medium-sized skillet over medium heat. Add canola oil and sauté the onions, mushrooms, and *Worthington® Vegetable Skallops®* until onion is clear and the mushrooms are tender. Add the potatoes and seasonings and let sauté a couple more minutes until the potatoes are golden brown. Remove from heat and set aside.

For the Omelet: Place all ingredients in a blender or food processor and process until smooth. Spray a medium skillet with a nonstick cooking spray and heat until medium hot. Pour in ½ cup of the omelet mixture and quickly spread out into a circle with the back of a spoon. Cook until firm. Flip over and cook the other side until golden brown. Remove from heat and fill with ½ cup of the filling. Serve warm with the lemon pesto drizzled over the top.

For the Pesto: Place all ingredients into a blender or food processor and process until smooth. You can add more water or olive oil if you want a thinner pesto.

This looks like a lot of steps, but I promise it is worth it! You can make the filling, pesto, and omelet the day before and then just fry up the omelet and heat up the filling before assembling. I like to garnish with fresh diced tomatoes. Since the filling makes 8 ½-cup servings, you can add more filling for your guests and family members who may be hearty eaters! —Cinda

Yield: 4 omelets; 24 tablespoons of pesto

(1 omelet) Calories 260 Total Fat 7g Saturated Fat 1g Sodium 780mg Total Carbohydrates 20g Fiber 6g Protein 28g
(1 tablespoon pesto) Calories 35 Total Fat 3.5g Saturated Fat 0g Sodium 75mg Total Carbohydrates <1g Fiber 0g Protein 1g

Florentine Mushroom Quiche

Spray a large skillet generously with a nonstick cooking spray. Sauté the onions and mushrooms on medium-low heat until the onions are clear. If they start to stick, then spray again with the nonstick cooking spray. Add the shredded spinach and stir to mix. Sauté for approximately one minute, just until slightly wilted. Remove from heat and add the potatoes and grated **Loma Linda® Linketts™**. Gently stir until evenly combined. Spray a 9 x 13 casserole dish with a nonstick cooking spray and add the vegetable mixture.

Place the remaining ingredients in the blender and blend on high until well blended. Pour over vegetables and gently stir until well mixed. Bake at 350 degrees for 45 minutes, or until it springs back when lightly touched. Remove from oven and let sit for 5 minutes, and then cut into 12 even squares. Serve warm.

This quiche can also be made into two 9-inch round plates if you prefer your quiche shaped in the traditional pie shape. It can also be assembled the day before and then baked the next day, which makes it nice for those busy mornings. —Cinda

1 medium onion, diced

2 cups fresh mushrooms, sliced

3 cups fresh spinach leaves, shredded

5 cups cooked potatoes, sliced

5 *Loma Linda® Linketts™*, shredded or grated

2 14-ounce packages firm, water-packed tofu

¾ cup cornstarch

1¼ cups water

3 tablespoons nutritional yeast flakes

1¼ teaspoons salt

½ teaspoon onion powder

¼ teaspoon nutmeg

¼ teaspoons dry mustard

2 tablespoons extra virgin olive oil

Yield: 12 squares

(1 square) Calories 210 Total Fat 7g Saturated Fat 1g Sodium 470mg Total Carbohydrates 24g Fiber 3g Protein 11g

Eggless Omelet

Filling:

2 cups frozen shredded potatoes

6 *Loma Linda® Linketts™*, sliced

½ teaspoon seasoned salt

Salt to taste

1 cup onions, diced fine

½ cup water

Omelet:

1 cup unbleached all-purpose flour

¼ teaspoon turmeric

½ teaspoon McKay's Chicken Style
    Seasoning

½ teaspoon granulated onion

¼ teaspoon salt

1½ cups unsweetened soymilk

7 vegan cheese slices

For the Filling: In a large skillet that has been sprayed with non-stick cooking spray, sauté the frozen shredded potatoes, *Loma Linda® Linketts™*, salt, and seasoned salt until golden brown. Place the onions and water in a covered glass dish and cook in the microwave on high for approximately 4 to 5 minutes or until onions are tender. Drain, then add to the potato mixture. Set aside till ready to use.

For the Omelet: In a medium-sized bowl, whisk the flour, seasonings, and soymilk together until smooth. Heat a small skillet over medium-high heat. Spray with nonstick cooking spray. Place ¼ cup of the batter in the hot pan and roll around moving in a fast circular motion until the pan is covered. As soon as it is firm, flip it on the other side. Place a cheese slice on top and spread ¼ cup of filling on top of the cheese Fold the omelet in half. When the cheese is melted, carefully flip it over for about another 10 to 15 seconds. Serve hot!

This is a delicious omelet that is very easy to make. The omelet without the filling can be made ahead of time. Just put plastic wrap between the omelets and refrigerate until ready to use. Serve with a fresh fruit salad and some homemade muffins. —Linda

Yield: 7 omelets

(1 omelet) Calories 280 Total Fat 11g Saturated Fat 3.5g Sodium 900mg Total Carbohydrates 31g Fiber 3g Protein 13g

Quinoa Breakfast Sausage

Crumble *MorningStar Farms®* Roasted Garlic and Quinoa Burgers and *MorningStar Farms® Grillers®* Chik'n Veggie Patties in a medium-sized bowl. Add the remaining ingredients and mix well. Form into 2½-inch patties and place on a baking sheet that has been sprayed with nonstick cooking spray, or on a Silpat nonstick baking liner.

Spray tops of patties with nonstick cooking spray. Bake at 400 degrees for 15 minutes, spray patties again, then flip and bake an additional 10 minutes. (Patties should be slightly crispy but moist and chewy inside.)

These are the tastiest little sausages that are so good your family and friends may think it's the "real thing"! You'll be amazed at the powerful punch of flavor with such few ingredients! Don't let the word "garlic" in the name of **MorningStar Farms®** *Roasted Garlic and Quinoa Burgers scare you off. There is just a subtle hint of garlic, and combined with the* **MorningStar Farms® Grillers®** *Chik'n Veggie Patties, they have a wonderful chewy texture too. My advice—double the recipe and save some for your freezer! —Brenda*

1 9.5-ounce package *MorningStar Farms®* Roasted Garlic and Quinoa Burgers

1 9.5-ounce package *MorningStar Farms® Grillers®* Chik'n Veggie Patties

3 tablespoons original Cholula hot sauce

½ cup silken tofu

½ cup quick oats

Yield: 11 sausages

(1 sausage) Calories 110 Total Fat 4.5g Saturated Fat 0.5g Sodium 360mg Total Carbohydrates 12g Fiber 5g Protein 8g

Sausage Burrito

2 14-ounce packages extra-firm water-packed tofu

1 tablespoon dehydrated onion

1 teaspoon fresh parsley

1 teaspoon turmeric

2 tablespoons McKay's Chicken Style Seasoning

½ teaspoon garlic powder

Salt to taste

1 19-ounce can *Loma Linda*® Little Links, sliced

12 whole-wheat tortillas

1½ cups ketchup

Drain and rinse tofu. Squeeze dry using a paper towel. Spray a skillet with nonstick cooking spray and heat over medium high. Add tofu and crumble with a spatula. Add onion, parsley, turmeric, McKay's Chicken Style Seasoning, garlic powder, and salt and mix well. Sauté until golden.

In a separate skillet that has been sprayed with nonstick cooking spray, sauté *Loma Linda*® Little Links over medium heat until browned on both sides. Add to tofu mixture.

Place a tortilla in a large skillet and warm on both sides. Place ½ cup tofu mixture in the center of each tortilla, top with 2 tablespoons ketchup, and fold like a burrito. Serve immediately.

I love Mexican food basically any time, but this burrito is great for breakfast at home or "on the go!" I prefer the whole-wheat, high-fiber tortillas, but you can use whatever brand is your favorite, or better yet, make your own! If making them for lunch, I suggest adding jalapeño nacho slices and guacamole! —Brenda

Yield: 12 burritos

(1 burrito) Calories 230 Total Fat 6g Saturated Fat 1g Sodium 550mg Total Carbohydrates 31g Fiber 4g Protein 13g

Sausage Biscuit Rollups

For the Filling: On medium-high heat in a medium-sized skillet that has been sprayed with nonstick cooking spray, place all the ingredients. Sauté until the onions are tender. Remove from heat and set aside.

For the Dough: In a medium-sized bowl, mix the white whole-wheat flour, baking powder, and salt together. Cut in the soy margarine with a pastry blender or fork until it forms small pieces. Gently stir in the soymilk until it is all blended together and forms a soft ball. Sprinkle about ¼ cup of flour on a clean counter. Roll out the dough until it is ½-inch thick. (If the rolling pin sticks to the dough, sprinkle a little flour on top.)

First spread the Tofutti Better Than Sour Cream on the dough and then top with the filling. Very carefully roll up the dough, patting it together if it starts to break apart. Slice into 16 1-inch pieces and place in a glass baking dish (or cookie sheet) that has been sprayed with nonstick cooking spray. Bake at 400 degrees for 20 to 25 minutes. Serve hot!

*Everyone loves biscuits and gravy, and this delicious dish is sure to be a favorite! I enjoy the **Loma Linda**® Little Links in a bun for lunch or supper but it is good for breakfast too! Serve it just like it is or with your favorite white gravy and garnish with baco bits. —Linda*

Filling:

1 cup onions, diced fine

½ teaspoon onion powder

2 cups potatoes, cooked and diced into small pieces

½ teaspoon seasoned salt

½ teaspoon salt

2 cups *Loma Linda*® Little Links, diced fine

1 teaspoon McKay's Chicken Style Seasoning

Biscuit Dough:

2 cups white whole-wheat flour

1 tablespoon baking powder

½ teaspoon salt

½ cup soy margarine

¾ cup soymilk

¼ cup Tofutti Better Than Sour Cream

Yield: 16 rollups

(1 rollup) Calories 170 Total Fat 8g Saturated Fat 1g Sodium 510mg Total Carbohydrates 19g Fiber 2g Protein 6g

Biscuit Burgers

3½ cups water

1 cup *Loma Linda® Redi-Burger™*

¼ cup Bragg Liquid Aminos

¼ cup nutritional yeast flakes

2 tablespoons canola oil

2 tablespoons onion powder

2–3 tablespoons maple syrup

1 tablespoon ground sage

1 tablespoon Italian seasoning

1½ teaspoons garlic powder

¼–½ teaspoon cayenne pepper, optional

3½ cups quick oats

Preheat oven to 350 degrees. Coat a baking sheet with nonstick cooking spray. Combine all ingredients, except oats, in a medium saucepan; bring to a boil over high heat. Remove from heat; add oats and stir well. Allow mixture to sit for 5 to 15 minutes. Form into ¼ cup patties; place on prepared baking sheet. Bake 15 minutes; flip and bake an additional 15 minutes. Serve on your favorite biscuits.

Monica Flower, the mother of three of our regulars on Tiny Tots, *Tyler, Tabitha, and Tori, made these and brought them to our apartment after a long day of taping. Linda and I loved them, and I asked her if I could put the recipe in our new cookbook. She graciously agreed and even let me modify the recipe a little. I love to eat them between flaky warm biscuits! They freeze well, so go ahead and make a double batch. —Cinda*

Yield: 22 burgers

(1 burger) Calories 80 Total Fat 2.5g Saturated Fat 0g Sodium 200mg Total Carbohydrates 11g Fiber 2g Protein 5g

Country Biscuits and Gravy

For Biscuits: Preheat oven to 450 degrees. Mix the almond milk and fresh lemon juice together and set aside. In a mixing bowl, mix the dry ingredients together. Add the cold soy margarine and cut in with a pastry blender or fork until it forms small pieces. Make a well in the dry ingredients and pour the milk in the middle. Stir gently with a wooden spoon until slightly combined. (The dough will be sticky.)

Turn onto a floured surface, dust the top with a bit of flour, and then gently turn the dough over on itself 5 or 6 times, gently kneading. Pat into a 1-inch thick circle and using a 2 ¾-inch round cutter (or any size circle cutter you prefer), cut into rounds and place on a baking sheet that has been sprayed with nonstick cooking spray, making sure they just touch. (This will help them rise uniformly.) Gently reform the dough and continue to cut into rounds until all the dough is cut. Spray the tops with a nonstick cooking spray or brush with melted soy margarine. Bake for 12 to 15 minutes or until fluffy and slightly golden brown. Remove from oven and serve hot with gravy.

For Gravy: In a medium saucepan, add the flour, almond milk, and salt. Stir with a whisk to mix well. Heat over medium heat until thick and bubbly, stirring constantly to avoid burning. Stir until thickened, about 2 minutes. Lower heat and add the grated *Loma Linda*® Little Links. Gently stir to combine and serve hot over biscuits.

Biscuits:

- 1 cup unsweetened original almond milk
- 1 tablespoon fresh lemon juice
- 2 cups whole-wheat flour
- 1 tablespoon baking powder
- ½ teaspoon baking soda
- ¾ teaspoon salt
- ¼ cup cold soy margarine

Gravy:

- ¾ cup Wondra flour, or a very finely ground flour
- 3½ cups original unsweetened almond milk
- 1½ teaspoons salt, or to taste
- 8 *Loma Linda*® Little Links, grated

Whenever I serve this, memories of Mom making us biscuits and gravy for breakfast when we were growing up come flooding back. I can see the table now, a plate stacked high with golden browned flaky biscuits warm from the oven, a big bowl of hot gravy, and a platter full of crispy fried potatoes! Treat your family to this delicious breakfast and create your own memories! —Cinda

Yield: 6 biscuits, 4 cups gravy

(1 biscuit and ⅔ cup gravy) Calories 280 Total Fat 11g Saturated Fat 1.5g Sodium 1540mg Total Carbohydrates 36g Fiber 7g Protein 13g

Veggie Medley Tarts

Filling:

2 cups potatoes, coarsely diced

¾ teaspoon Vegesal, or favorite vegetable seasoned salt

1 medium onion, diced

½ teaspoon red pepper flakes (optional)

2 cups mushrooms, sliced

½ teaspoon parsley

2 *Gardenburger Veggie Medley®* Veggie Burgers , crumbled

Crust:

1¼ cups all purpose flour

½ teaspoon salt

⅓ cup canola oil

3 tablespoons original almond milk

2–4 tablespoons ketchup

For Filling: Preheat oven to 400 degrees. Spray a baking sheet with nonstick cooking spray. Layer the potatoes evenly on the tray. Spray the tops with nonstick cooking spray, then sprinkle with Vegesal or your favorite vegetable seasoned salt. Bake until tender and golden, approximately 15 minutes, flipping once during cooking.

In a large skillet that has been sprayed with nonstick cooking spray, sauté onions over medium-high heat until they are clear. Add red pepper flakes and mushrooms. Continue sautéing until tender. Add parsley, crumbled burgers, and potatoes. Sauté an additional 3 to 4 minutes. Set aside.

For Crust: Mix dry ingredients together in a small bowl, set aside. In a separate small bowl, mix oil and milk together with fork till well blended. Pour liquid mixture into flour mixture and blend quickly with rubber spatula until all flour is absorbed and forms a ball. (If necessary, add a small amount of additional flour).

On a pastry mat, roll the dough out into a 9 x 11 rectangle and cut into six equal pieces, then place each one in a muffin tin. Fill with ½ cup of potato mixture. Drizzle each with 1 to 2 teaspoons ketchup and bake at 425 degrees for 20 to 25 minutes or until crust is golden.

*These tarts are great for breakfast, but also wonderful for appetizers too. Just make them in smaller muffin tins to make them bite-size. The **Gardenburger Veggie Medley**® Veggie Burgers crumble easily and give just the right flavor. For a touch more heat, add ¼ cup jalapeño nacho slices. —Brenda*

Yield: 6 tarts

(1 tart) Calories 360 Total Fat 14g Saturated Fat 1g Sodium 810mg Total Carbohydrates 52g Fiber 7g Protein 9g

Belgian Breakwich

For Waffles: In a small mixing bowl, mix the flaxseed meal with the water and let sit for 5 minutes until thickened. In a large mixing bowl, add the remaining ingredients and whisk gently until just combined. Let batter rest while preheating your waffle iron. If you do not have a Belgian waffle iron, then you can use the regular one. Once preheated, generously spray the waffle iron with a nonstick cooking spray and spoon ½ cup of batter into the center of the waffle iron and cook until browned and crisp on the outside. When done, place on a cooling rack briefly to let steam roll off, then transfer to an ovenproof platter and keep warm in a 200-degree oven until ready to assemble your sandwich. Repeat until all the batter is used.

For Pesto: Place all ingredients in a small bowl and mix well.

For Sandwich: Thaw the *Gardenburger Veggie Medley*® Veggie Burgers and place in a hot skillet until browned on both sides, then remove and set aside. Place the tomato slices in the hot skillet, sprinkle with a little salt and sear on both sides. Remove and set aside. Spray the hot skillet generously with a nonstick cooking spray and sauté the fresh baby spinach, stirring gently until wilted. Remove from heat. Place a *Gardenburger Veggie Medley*® Veggie Burgers on one of the waffles and then put a tomato slice on top. Place half of the wilted spinach leaves on top of the tomato and drizzle with the pesto aioli. Place another waffle on the top and drizzle the top waffle with more of the pesto aioli. Repeat with other two waffles. Serve warm.

I made this for my husband, Joel, and he really enjoyed it! He put extra pesto aioli on his and, of course—a little hot sauce! You can serve this for breakfast, brunch, or supper. The waffle recipe can be doubled or even tripled, and they can also be made ahead of time and kept in the freezer until ready to thaw and use. Just pop them in the toaster until warm and crisp and then assemble your sandwich. —Cinda

Yield: 2 breakwiches; 12 tablespoons pesto

Waffles:

- 1 tablespoon flaxseed meal
- 2½ tablespoons water
- ½ cup unsweetened applesauce
- 1 tablespoon grapeseed oil
- ½ tablespoon baking powder
- ¼ teaspoon salt
- 1 tablespoon brown sugar
- ½ teaspoon cinnamon
- ¾ cup original unsweetened almond milk
- 1 cup whole-wheat flour
- ¼ cup white whole-wheat flour

Pesto Aioli:

- ½ cup Reduced Fat Vegenaise
- ¼ cup pesto
- 2 teaspoons original unsweetened almond milk

Sandwich:

- 2 *Gardenburger Veggie Medley*® Veggie Burgers
- 2 thick slices fresh tomatoes
- 2 cups fresh baby spinach leaves

(½ breakwich) Calories 260 Total Fat 7g Saturated Fat 0.5g Sodium 560mg Total Carbohydrates 45g Fiber 8g Protein 8g

(1 tablespoon pesto) Calories 50 Total Fat 6g Saturated Fat 0g Sodium 105mg Total Carbohydrates <1g Fiber 0g Protein 0g

Pancake Poppers

1 cup whole-wheat flour

1 cup white whole-wheat flour

2 teaspoons baking powder

½ teaspoon baking soda

½ teaspoon salt

¼ cup applesauce

1 tablespoon pure maple syrup

1½ cups vanilla almond milk

1 19-ounce can *Loma Linda*® Little Links

Mix all of the dry ingredients together in a medium-sized mixing bowl and stir to combine. Add the applesauce, pure maple syrup, and the almond milk and stir to mix well.

Cut *Loma Linda*® Little Links into 7 slices each, then add to the pancake mix. Heat a large skillet over medium heat and spray with a nonstick cooking spray. Pour ⅓ cup of batter into the skillet for each pancake. Cook until golden brown on both sides. Serve hot with vegan margarine and pure maple syrup.

I served these to my husband for a light supper one evening when he had been working late and did not want to eat a heavy meal. He loved them! They were great served with some fresh fruit. Of course he also thinks they would be great served for breakfast or brunch! —Cinda

Yield: 14 pancakes

(1 pancake) Calories 140 Total Fat 4g Saturated Fat 0.5g Sodium 340mg Total Carbohydrates 18g Fiber 2g Protein 7g

Sunshine Strudel

Spray a skillet with nonstick cooking spray. Add potatoes, ½ teaspoon salt, and parsley and cook over medium-high heat until potatoes are browned. Set aside.

Slice **Worthington® Vegetable Steaks™** in half, then in half again. Dredge in flour. Sauté over medium high in a skillet that has been sprayed with nonstick cooking spray until they are golden brown on both sides, spraying the tops of the steaks before flipping them. In a separate skillet that has been sprayed with nonstick cooking spray, sauté onion until clear. Add peppers, red pepper flakes, and the remainder of the salt, and sauté until peppers are tender. Add steaks.

Roll out crescent roll dough. Slice from edge toward the middle at 1-inch intervals, leaving 3 inches in the center that is not cut. Line center of dough with steak filling. Lift cut sections over the top alternating from side to side. Lightly press strips together in the center.

Bake at 375 degrees for 10 to 15 minutes or until golden brown.

This recipe is great for a breakfast buffet and is one of those "wow" recipes for special events. You can easily convert to individual "Steaks in a Blanket" by cutting dough in small sections and placing in a muffin tin, adding ⅓ cup of the filling mixture to each muffin cup, and bring points of dough together, pinching to seal. Bake for the same amount of time or until golden. —Brenda

- 1 cup cooked red potatoes, diced fine
- 1½ teaspoons salt
- 1 teaspoon parsley
- 1 cup **Worthington® Vegetable Steaks™**
- 1 medium onion, slivered
- 1 cup sweet yellow pepper, slivered
- ¼ cup petite diced tomatoes, drained
- 1 teaspoon red pepper flakes
- 1 can refrigerated seamless crescent rolls

Yield: 8 slices

(1 slice) Calories 80 Total Fat 1.5g Saturated Fat 0.5g Sodium 660mg Total Carbohydrates 11g Fiber 2g Protein 6g

Good Morning Pizza

Filling:
2 cups cooked potatoes, diced

Salt to taste

½ teaspoon seasoned salt

1 20-ounce can *Loma Linda®* Big Franks

2 cups onion, finely diced

½ cup water

Crust:
⅔ cup canola oil

5 tablespoons ice water

2 cups unbleached white flour

½ teaspoon salt

½ cup Tofutti Better Than Sour Cream

Vegan cheese (optional)

Ketchup

For Filling: In a large skillet that has been sprayed with nonstick cooking spray, add the potatoes and seasonings and sauté until golden brown over medium-high heat. Add the sliced *Loma Linda®* Big Franks and sauté for another 5 to 10 minutes. Place the onions and water in a covered glass dish in the microwave and cook on high for approximately 4 to 6 minutes or until onions are tender. Drain the excess water off and add to potato mixture.

For Crust: In a small bowl, whip briskly together the canola oil and ice water until it turns white. In a medium-sized bowl, mix the flour and salt together and slowly add the oil mixture to the flour. Gently stir until all the liquid is folded in. With a rolling pin, roll the dough out between two pieces of wax paper into the size of a 12-inch pizza pan. Spray the pizza pan with nonstick cooking spray. Remove the top piece of wax paper and lay the pizza pan upside down on it. Flip the pan over and pull the other piece of wax paper off and flute the edges of the crust all the way around.

Spread the bottom of the pizza crust with the Tofutti Better Than Sour Cream and then top with the filling. Sprinkle vegan cheddar cheese on top and bake at 400 degrees for 20 to 25 minutes. Remove from oven and drizzle with ketchup. Serve hot.

To add a bit of spice, try adding ½ teaspoon of red pepper flakes sautéed with the filling. The pizza crust can be made ahead and put into the freezer unbaked so it is ready for that special breakfast. Serve with a fresh fruit salad and a good appetite! —Linda

Yield: 12 3-inch slices

(1 slice) Calories 370 Total Fat 16g Saturated Fat 1g Sodium 520mg Total Carbohydrates 45g Fiber 5g Protein 13g

Appetizers

Big Frank Hummus

1 16-ounce can garbanzo beans, drained, reserve the liquid

1 clove fresh garlic, minced

2 tablespoons fresh lemon juice

2 tablespoons tahini

½ teaspoon salt, or to taste

1 tablespoon extra virgin olive oil

½ cup liquid from the garbanzo beans

1 20-ounce can *Loma Linda*® Big Franks, drained, reserve the liquid

2 tablespoons liquid from the canned Big Franks

⅔ cup sweet pickle relish

Place all ingredients, except the pickle relish into a food processor, and blend until smooth. You can adjust the consistency by adding more of the reserved liquid from either the garbanzo beans or *Loma Linda*® Big Franks. Remove from processor into a bowl and stir in the sweet pickle relish. Serve at room temperature or refrigerate until needed.

When I presented this recipe to a group of friends it was an instant hit! They started thinking of all kinds of creative ways they would serve this hummus. As a dip, sandwich spread, in small appetizer cups, in hollowed out thick slices of cucumber and even stuffed in olives. Make a batch of this yourself and see what creative ways you can come up with! —Cinda

Yield: 20 ¼-cup servings

(¼ cup) Calories 80 Total Fat 3g Saturated Fat 0g Sodium 290mg Total Carbohydrates 7g Fiber 2g Protein 6g

Chik'n Salad Dip

Crumble thawed **MorningStar Farms® Grillers®** Chik'n Veggie Patties in a medium-sized bowl. Add remaining ingredients and mix well.

This Chick'n Salad Dip is a favorite with my family! I serve it with tortilla chips, but this dip is also good as a spread on whole-wheat buns, bread, crackers, and pita breads. It is a great appetizer for parties or as a light evening meal at home. Just add a fresh fruit salad and invite some family and friends over for a fun evening! —Linda

1 9.5-ounce package **MorningStar Farms® Grillers®** Chik'n Veggie Patties

¼ cup sweet red pepper, finely diced

¼ cup dill pickle slices, finely diced

¼ cup carrots, finely grated

¼ cup Grapeseed Vegenaise

pinch cayenne pepper

⅛ teaspoon onion powder

⅛ teaspoon seasoned salt

Yield: 8 ¼-cup servings

(¼ cup) Calories 70 Total Fat 4g Saturated Fat 0g Sodium 300mg Total Carbohydrates 5g Fiber 2g Protein 4g

Black Bean Chipotle Dip

1 tablespoon olive oil

¾ cup onion, finely diced

½ teaspoon red pepper flakes

2 cloves garlic, minced fine

4 cups canned tomatoes

¼ cup red pepper, finely chopped

¼ teaspoon salt

2 teaspoons chili powder

1 10-ounce package *Gardenburger*® Black Bean Chipotle Veggie Burgers

1 15-ounce can black beans, drained

1 tablespoon jalapeño nacho slices

In a medium-sized skillet over medium heat, sauté onion, red pepper flakes, and garlic in olive oil till onions are clear. Add tomatoes, red peppers, salt, and chili powder and stir till tomatoes are broken up. Add the *Gardenburger*® Black Bean Chipotle Veggie Burgers, black beans, and jalapeño slices. Simmer for approximately 10 to 15 minutes more. Remove from heat. Place ½ cup of the cooked mixture in the blender and process until smooth. Mix with the remainder of the dip, stirring well. Serve this appetizer with tortilla chips.

My aunt Myrtle said that this Black Bean Chipotle Dip is her absolute favorite, and she gives it a 10! This appetizer is very versatile and can be used to make nachos or quesadillas and is a great filling for burritos. It's sure to be a hit at any gathering! —Linda

Yield 20 ¼-cup servings

(¼ cup) Calories 60 Total Fat 1.5g Saturated Fat 0g Sodium 260mg Total Carbohydrates 10g Fiber 3g Protein 1.5g

Garden Stuffed Mushrooms

Wash mushrooms. Scoop out the stem with a spoon and reserve in a bowl. Place mushroom caps on a baking sheet that has been lined with aluminum foil.

Dice stems and place in a skillet that has been sprayed with nonstick cooking spray. Add onions, garlic, parsley, and sage and sauté over medium-high heat until onions are clear. Crumble **Gardenburger Veggie Medley**® Veggie Burgers and add to the skillet with remaining ingredients. Mix well. Scoop approximately 2 to 3 tablespoons into the hollow part of each mushroom cap.

Place in an oven that has been preheated to 375 degrees. Bake for 20 to 25 minutes.

*Stuffed Mushrooms has always been one of my "go to" recipes when needing appetizers for an event. These actually taste very similar to the traditional ones with just a slight difference, as I have added the **Gardenburger Veggie Medley**® Veggie Burgers. I not only like the flavor but I love the added healthy veggies and not just all the carbs of the stuffing! You can use whatever seasoned bread crumbs you like, but my favorite is the Pepperidge Farms brand because of the seasonings in the crumbs. (If using unseasoned bread crumbs, you'll need to add extra seasonings of your own. I suggest using onion powder, garlic powder, and sage—just be creative.) —Brenda*

24 extra large baking mushrooms

1 medium onion, diced

1 clove garlic, minced

1 teaspoon parsley

1 teaspoon sage

4 cups fresh spinach

1 10-ounce package *Gardenburger Veggie Medley*® Veggie Burgers

2 cups Pepperidge Farm Stuffing Mix

2 tablespoons McKay's Chicken Style Seasoning

2 cups water

Yield: 24 stuffed mushrooms

(1 mushroom) Calories 60 Total Fat 1g Saturated Fat 0g Sodium 260mg Total Carbohydrates 11g Fiber 2g Protein 3g

Potato Pierogi Bites

Wonton Wraps:

7 ⅓ cups all-purpose flour

1¾ teaspoon salt

1¾ cups warm water

Filling:

1 medium onion, diced

2 tablespoons soy margarine

3 cups cooked potatoes, diced, kept warm

1 19-ounce can *Loma Linda*® Little Links, grated

½–1 teaspoon VegeSal (or to taste)

For Wonton Wraps: Mix flour and salt together in a mixing bowl, and then slowly add the warm water. Knead on a floured surface until dough is smooth, approximately 10 minutes. Dough will be stiff. Cover and let sit for 15 to 20 minutes. Roll out very thin and cut into 3-inch squares. Store in an airtight container in the refrigerator or freezer.

For Filling: In a medium skillet, sauté the onion with the margarine over low-medium heat until the onion is clear. Add the remaining ingredients together and gently stir to thoroughly mix. The warm potatoes will mash slightly when stirred.

Place 1 to 2 tablespoons of mixture into the middle of a wonton wrapper. Dip your finger in a bowl of water and moisten the edges of the wrapper. Place another wonton wrapper on top and firmly press all the edges to seal them. Repeat with the rest of the wonton wrappers.

Bring a pan of salted water to a boil, and then lower the heat to a simmer. Carefully slip the pierogi into the water, letting it simmer gently, and cook for approximately 2 minutes, until tender. Using a slotted spoon, remove the pierogi from the water and drain. Place on a serving platter and drizzle each one with melted vegan margarine. Place a small dollop of vegan sour cream on top of each pierogi and garnish with chopped parsley. Serve warm or at room temperature.

I have always loved pierogi. When Joel and I were first married, we lived in Pittsburg, PA. They have many different ethnic sections to that city, and one of my favorites was the Polish community near Squirrel Hill. There they make the pierogi fresh with tender homemade dough that literally melts in your mouth. Whenever we go back for a visit, I bring a big cooler so that I can take some back home to Tennessee with me! These pierogi are easy to make and, while not as good as the ones in Pittsburgh, they are delicious in their own right and make a great appetizer. You can also serve them for dinner with your favorite sauce. —Cinda

Yield: 55 pierogi (110 3-inch wonton squares)

(1 pierogi) Calories 90 Total Fat 1.5g Saturated Fat 0g Sodium 125mg Total Carbohydrates 15g Fiber <1g Protein 3g

Veggie Dog Sushi

Bring the rice, water, salt, soy sauce, and vegetable seasoning to a boil in a saucepan over high heat. Reduce heat to medium low, cover, and simmer until the rice is tender and the liquid has been absorbed, approximately 20 to 25 minutes. Let stand, covered, for approximately 10 minutes to absorb any excess water. Set rice aside to cool.

To roll the sushi, lay a sheet of roasted seaweed, rough side up, on plastic wrap. With wet fingers, firmly pat ½ cup of prepared rice over the seaweed, covering it completely. Place approximately 1 tablespoon each of cucumber, red pepper, avocado, and **Loma Linda**® Big Franks in a line along the bottom edge of the seaweed. Roll the bottom edge of the sheet up, enclosing the filling, and tightly roll the sushi into a thick cylinder. Once the sushi is rolled, gently squeeze to compact it tightly. Cut each roll into 6 pieces and refrigerate until served.

My brother Ken makes the best sushi rolls and gave me the idea for these tasty appetizers. I like to dip them in different sauces, but they are good just like they are. They make great appetizers for any occasion! —Linda

3 cups sushi rice

1 teaspoon Bragg Liquid Aminos

1 teaspoon salt

1 teaspoon oriental vegetable seasoning – No MSG

4 sheets roasted seaweed

½ cup cucumbers, cut into thin strips

1 cup sweet red pepper, diced

1 avocado, cut into slices

1 cup *Loma Linda*® Big Franks, sliced in long strips

Yield: 24 1-inch pieces

(1 piece) Calories 100 Total Fat 0.5g Saturated Fat 0g Sodium 210mg Total Carbohydrates 19g Fiber <1g Protein 4g

Sriracha Hot Dog Poppers

1 8-ounce can Reduced Fat Pillsbury Crescent Dinner Rolls

4 *Loma Linda® Linketts™*, cut in half

Sriracha sauce to taste

½ cup vegan shredded cheddar cheese

Yellow cornmeal

Heat oven to 375 degrees. Unroll crescent roll dough and separate into the 8 triangles. Place a *Loma Linda® Linketts™* half in the middle of each triangle. Place a desired amount (depending on how spicy you want) of Sriracha sauce on top of and around the hot dog and sprinkle with 1 tablespoon of the vegan shredded cheese. Gather up sides to completely cover the hot dog and pinch edges to seal. Place on a baking sheet that has been lined with parchment paper. Spray with a nonstick cooking spray and sprinkle with the yellow cornmeal. Bake for 12 to 13 minutes or until lightly browned. Serve warm or at room temperature.

These were a big hit with all of my taste testers! They are great to serve at parties because they can be eaten at room temperature. You can also use ketchup in place of the Sriracha sauce for those who don't like spicy. —Cinda

Yield: 8 poppers

(1 popper) Calories 130 Total Fat 7g Saturated Fat 2.5g Sodium 300mg Total Carbohydrates 13g Fiber <1g Protein 6g

Ball Park Pinwheels

Drain **Loma Linda® Linketts**™ and pulse in a food processor until mashed or use a fork or hand masher. Place in small bowl, then add remaining ingredients, except dough.

Open the can of biscuit dough and separate. Roll out each biscuit to 4 x 6. Spread 2 to 3 tablespoons filling mixture evenly on top. Roll up like a jelly roll and slice into 6 equal pieces. Place on a baking sheet that has been lined with parchment paper, or use a Silpat baking mat. Bake at 400 degrees for 10 minutes.

*I've been making pinwheel appetizers for years but the secret ingredient that makes this recipe so special is definitely the **Loma Linda® Linketts**™! My grandsons, Michael and Jason, love **Loma Linda® Linketts**™ so much that they think it isn't a meal without them. So of course both boys gave this recipe a "two thumbs up," calling it "cookbook worthy"! I also love the flavor the Cholula sauce adds. This sauce packs a lot of flavor and just a mild amount of heat. If you don't have any, you can substitute any hot sauce of your choice.*
—Brenda

1 20-ounce can *Loma Linda® Linketts*™

¼ cup onion, finely diced

1 clove garlic, minced

1 4-ounce can chopped green chilies

2 tablespoons jalapeño nacho slices, diced

1 tablespooon original Cholula sauce

1 teaspoon chili powder

½ cup green olives, sliced

1 teaspoon agave nectar

1 can refrigerated biscuit dough

Yield: 48 pinwheels

(1 pinwheel) Calories 30 Total Fat 1.5g Saturated Fat 0g Sodium 120mg Total Carbohydrates 3g Fiber <1g Protein 2g

Egg Salad Bites

1 medium onion, diced

1 cup *Loma Linda*® Tender Bits, diced fine

1 14-ounce package extra firm water-packed tofu, drained and rinsed

½ teaspoon onion powder

2 tablespoons McKay's Chicken Style Seasoning

1 teaspoon turmeric

½ teaspoon Lawrey's Seasoning Salt

½ cup Grapeseed Vegenaise

¼ cup bread and butter pickles, diced fine

18 slices whole wheat bread, crusts removed

Add onions and *Loma Linda*® Tender Bits to a skillet that has been sprayed with nonstick cooking spray. Sauté over medium heat until onions are clear. Pat dry the tofu, then crumble. Add to skillet, along with onion powder, McKay's Chicken Style Seasoning, and turmeric. Sauté until tofu is dry, but not golden. Spread on baking sheet to cool.

Once cool, place in medium-sized mixing bowl. Sprinkle Lawrey's on top, then add Vegenaise and sweet pickles. Mix well.

Spread ¼ cup on 9 slices of bread. Top with another slice. Cut into four triangles.

You'll be surprised at how much these taste like real "egg" salad sandwiches! You can replace the bread and butter pickles with sweet pickle relish using exact amounts. I honestly like both and don't have a preference. This filling works well on top of crackers or mini hard breads or on any small petite-size fresh bread. Garnish with a sliced black olive, radish slices, or pimento. I've made mini pita pockets with it and that works too. If you don't need appetizers, use this filling for sandwiches at lunchtime! —Brenda

Yield: 36 sandwich triangles

(¼ sandwich) Calories 60 Total Fat 2.5g Saturated Fat 0g Sodium 230mg Total Carbohydrates 6g Fiber <1g Protein 4g

Mini Chili Cups

Open the can of crescent dough, unroll it, and divide it into the precut 8 triangles. Cut each triangle in half.

Spray a mini tart/muffin tin with a nonstick cooking spray and place the pieces of dough into each of the muffin tins, forming them into a cup. Empty the *Worthington* Chili into a small bowl and stir well. Fill each cup with 1 tablespoon of the *Worthington* Chili. Bake at 375 degrees for 11 to 14 minutes or until the dough is golden brown. Remove from oven and let cool for 1 minute before removing from pan. Eat warm or at room temperature.

I made this for Brenda's grandsons when they were over swimming at my house, and they loved them! They are a filling and easy snack that the boys were able to eat with their hands. You can put some vegan cheese on top of them or some crushed corn chips if you are serving them to your guests for an appetizer. The boys preferred them just warm right out of the oven and told me they didn't need for me to "decorate them"! —Cinda

1 cup *Worthington* Chili

1 8-ounce can Pillsbury Reduced Fat Crescent Dough

Yield: 16 mini cups

(1 chili cup) Calories 60 Total Fat 3g Saturated Fat 1g Sodium 180mg Total Carbohydrates 8g Fiber <1g Protein 2g

Teeny Tiny Tacos

¼ cup onion, diced

1 10-ounce package *Gardenburger*® Black Bean Chipotle Veggie Burgers, crumbled

1 package Baked Tostitos or another kind of baked scooped tortilla chip

1 medium avocado, sliced

Sauté onion in a skillet that has been sprayed with nonstick cooking spray over medium-high heat until clear. Add *Gardenburger*® Black Bean Chipotle Veggie Burgers and sauté until browned. Fill each tortilla scoop with 1 teaspoon burger mix. Top each taco with an avocado slice.

This is an easy recipe because there's not a lot of prep time and few ingredients. You can make up the filling mixture the night before and heat just prior to filling the scooped tortilla chips. I like to garnish with more than one garnish. Some of my favorites are black olive slices, jalapeño nacho slices, or a dollop of guacamole on top! —*Brenda*

Yield: 72 teeny tiny tacos

(4 tacos) Calories 100 Total Fat 3g Saturated Fat 0g Sodium 150mg Total Carbohydrates 16g Fiber 3g Protein 3g

Spinach Triangles

Sauté onions and mushrooms in a skillet that has been sprayed with nonstick cooking spray over medium hot until onions are clear. Drain off any excess liquid. Add spinach, salt, McKay's Chicken Seasoning, red pepper flakes, cayenne, and diced **MorningStar Farms® Grillers®** Chik'n Veggie Patties.

Unroll the fillo dough on a flat surface and keep it covered with waxed paper and a damp towel so it doesn't dry out and become brittle. Using a sharp knife, cut the fillo into 3 x 11-inch strips and cover with the towel. Separate two strips of fillo dough and spray with nonstick cooking spray. Place one tablespoon of spinach filling 1 inch from the end of the pastry. Fold the end over the filling to form a triangle, then continue to fold up the strip in triangles, like folding up a flag. Continue with remaining strips of dough, placing filled triangles on the baking sheet and keeping them covered with a towel until all are ready to bake.

Spray the tops of each with nonstick cooking spray, then bake for 7 to 10 minutes at 400 degrees or until golden and crisp. Serve hot.

*Hands down, this is my husband Tim's all-time favorite appetizer! He loves these so much that sometimes I make them as part of his meal, even if we don't have guests. The **MorningStar Farms® Grillers®** Chik'n Veggie Patties gives this recipe all the seasoning it needs so there's not much more that I add. Be sure and keep any unused portion of fillo dough covered—only exposing the amount that you are working with. Otherwise, when it dries out, it becomes flaky and will break when trying to fold. —Brenda*

Ingredients

- 1 medium onion, coarsely chopped
- 3 cups fresh mushrooms, coarsely chopped
- 7 cups fresh baby spinach
- 1 teaspoon salt
- 1 tablespoon McKay's Chicken Style Seasoning
- 1 teaspoon red pepper flakes
- ¼ teaspoon cayenne
- 1 9.5-ounce package *MorningStar Farms® Grillers®* Chik'n Veggie Patties, diced
- ½ cup silken tofu
- 1 16-ounce package fillo dough

Yield: 27 triangles

(1 triangle) Calories 70 Total Fat 1.5g Saturated Fat 0g Sodium 280mg Total Carbohydrates 11g Fiber <1g Protein 3g

Lil' Chik'n Hot Pockets

1 19-ounce can *Loma Linda®* Tender Bits

½ cup Tofutti Better Than Cream Cheese

1 teaspoon crushed red pepper flakes

½ cup celery, diced

½ cup fresh spinach, shredded

½ teaspoon VegeSal

3 8-ounce packages Pillsbury Reduced Fat Crescent dough

Drain the **Loma Linda®** Tender Bits and place them in a food processor. Process until coarsely ground. Remove and place in a large mixing bowl. Add the remaining ingredients, except dough, and stir to thoroughly combine.

Unroll the crescent dough and separate into the pre-cut triangles. Place a generous tablespoon of filling in the middle of the triangle and gather the dough up around the filling to completely cover it and form a little pouch. Pinch edges to seal. Repeat using all of the filling and dough. Place on a baking sheet that has been sprayed with nonstick cooking spray and bake at 375 degrees for 10 to 12 minutes, or until golden brown. Remove from oven and let sit for 3 to 5 minutes to cool a little before eating.

I love cooking for Brenda's grandsons because they are usually quite picky eaters, and so if they like it . . . I know everyone else will! Michael and Jason love to spend the day at Aunt Ceda and Uncle Joel's farm, playing with the animals and tromping through the woods. All the outdoor activity makes them hungry and so I am always trying to think of quick, easy, and healthy foods they can have for a snack. (There is way too much fun to be had on the farm, so they don't want to waste time sitting down to eat!) They each grabbed several of these little hot pockets and went running off into the woods, only to reappear minutes later asking for more! —Cinda

Yield: 24 hot pockets

(1 hot pocket) Calories 120 Total Fat 6g Saturated Fat 2.5g Sodium 340mg Total Carbohydrates 14g Fiber <1g Protein 4g

Vegetable Sopes

For Dough: In a medium bowl, combine corn masa and salt. Add the water and mix quickly with your hands and knead until mixture forms a ball. Divide into 24 portions of 2 tablespoons and shape each portion into a ball. Heat a large griddle or skillet over medium-low heat; shape each ball into a 3½-inch circle and place on the ungreased griddle. Let cook for 2 to 3 minutes or until lightly browned and then turn over and cook the other side. Remove from the heat; quickly pinch edge of circles to form a ½-inch rim. Return to griddle and cook anther 2 minutes or until bottom is golden. Remove and put on wire cooling racks. Repeat with remaining dough.

For Filling: Spray a medium-sized skillet with nonstick cooking spray. Over medium heat, sauté the onion until clear. Add the garlic, salt, zucchini, corn, and *Gardenburger*® Black Bean Chipotle Veggie Burgers and continue to sauté until the zucchini is tender.

Place a teaspoon of pepper jelly or agave nectar in the bottom of each sope, then top it with a tablespoon of the vegetable filling. Garnish with a fresh cilantro or parsley leaf. Serve at room temperature.

Dough

2 cups instant corn masa flour

1 teaspoon salt

2 cups water

Vegetable Filling

1 small onion, finely chopped

3 cloves fresh garlic, minced

Salt to taste

2 cups zucchini, cut into small cubes

1 cup frozen corn kernels

1 10-ounce package *Gardenburger*® Black Bean Chipotle Veggie Burgers, crumbled

½ cup pepper jelly or agave nectar

When my husband was in college, he lived with one of his friends, Frank Martinez and his family, during the summer while he worked to earn money for his tuition. Frank's mother would get up early every morning and make them fresh tortillas for their lunches. Frank and his mother, Alicia, recently came to visit us, and she made Joel and me tamales, tortillas, and vegetable sopes. They were so delicious that I had to come up with a recipe to share with you all. I know you are going to love them as much as we do! —Cinda

Yield: 24 sopes

(1 sope) Calories 80 Total Fat 1g Saturated Fat 0g Sodium 160mg Total Carbohydrates 17g Fiber 2g Protein 2g

Steak Bowl Bites

9 slices whole-wheat bread

1 cup flour

¾ cup nutritional yeast flakes

1 20-ounce can *Worthington® Vegetable Steaks™*

2 medium onions, slivered

1–2 tablespoons soy margarine, melted

Ranch Dressing:

½ cup Reduced Fat Vegenaise

¼ teaspoon garlic powder

¼ teaspoon onion powder

½ teaspoon dried marjoram

1 teaspoon dried parsley

2 tablespoons original soymilk or almond milk

To prepare mini bread bowls, trim the crust off of each piece of bread and flatten with a rolling pin. Cut each piece into fourths. Spray the insides of each 2-inch mini muffin tin and gently place the squares of bread into them. Bake in a 350 degree oven for about 10 minutes or until lightly toasted and browned. Remove from oven and set aside.

In a medium plastic bag or bowl, mix the flour and nutritional yeast flakes together. Slice the *Worthington® Vegetable Steaks™* into medium to thin slices and place them in the bag of flour. Seal shut and shake until all *Worthington® Vegetable Steaks™* are well coated (or dip each piece in the bowl of flour mixture until well coated). Place *Worthington® Vegetable Steaks™* on a large baking sheet that has been sprayed with nonstick cooking spray. Spray the tops with the nonstick cooking spray and bake in a 375 degree oven for 15 minutes. Remove from oven, turn each of the *Worthington® Vegetable Steaks™* over, and return to oven for another 15 minutes. Remove from oven and cut each vegetable steak into bite-sized pieces.

Toss the onions with the melted soy margarine and place in a glass pie plate or microwavable dish. Microwave on high until onions are clear, stirring occasionally.

Toss the steaks with the cooked onions and add a tablespoon of mixture to the prepared mini bread bowls. Drizzle with the homemade Ranch dressing and serve hot or room temperature.

For Ranch Dressing: Mix all ingredients together in a medium bowl until well blended. Refrigerate until ready to use.

This appetizer was a big hit with all of my guests. Some thought they were delicious even without the ranch dressing! So you can serve them with just a simple garnish like a sprinkle of herbs if you prefer, or you could top them with a spicy tomato chutney for a little more pizzazz! —*Cinda*

Yield: 36 steak bowl bites

(1 steak bowl bite) Calories 60 Total Fat 1.5g Saturated Fat 0g Sodium 100mg Total Carbohydrates 7g Fiber <1g Protein 4g

Thai Lettuce Wraps

In a skillet that has been sprayed with nonstick cooking spray, sauté onion until clear. Add **Worthington® Vegetable Skallops®**. Continue sautéing until **Worthington® Vegetable Skallops®** are browned. Add garlic, ginger, and McKay's Chicken Style Seasoning. Add remaining ingredients and mix well. Simmer only until sauce starts to thicken. Serve with lettuce leaves, lime wedges, and crushed peanuts.

*My sister Cinda was the first one that introduced me to lettuce wraps, and I've been hooked ever since. In fact, I could eat them just about any time of day. I chose **Worthington® Vegetable Skallops®** for this recipe because it has a nice texture and doesn't have a strong flavor, so it takes on whatever flavor is in the dish. Don't skip the lime wedges as it is like "icing on the cake" and really adds to your whole tasting experience! —Brenda*

1 medium onion, chopped

1 20-ounce can *Worthington® Vegetable Skallops®*, diced

1 clove garlic, minced

1 teaspoon fresh ginger, minced

1 tablespoon McKay's Chicken Style Seasoning

½ cup peanut butter

1 cup water

1 tablespoon Bragg Liquid Aminos

5 teaspoons fresh lemon juice

3 tablespoons sweet chili sauce

1 tablespoon roasted red chili paste

Lettuce

Lime wedges

Crushed peanuts

Yield: 18 ¼-cup servings

(¼ cup filling) Calories 80 Total Fat 5g Saturated Fat 1g Sodium 230mg Total Carbohydrates 6g Fiber <1g Protein 3g

Mediterranean Sliders

½ cup water

2 teaspoons McKay's Chicken Style Seasoning

1 medium onion, diced

1 9.5-ounce package *MorningStar Farms® Grillers®* Chik'n Veggie Patties

2 15-ounce cans garbanzo beans, drained and rinsed

½ cup red bell pepper, chopped

½ cup kalamata olives, chopped

2 cups fresh spinach, chopped

1 cup quick oats

1 teaspoon dried or fresh oregano

½ teaspoon salt

½ cup pepperoncini, diced

½ cup bread crumbs, seasoned or plain

24 mini pita pockets, halved

Cucumber Sauce

1½ cups Tofutti Better Than Sour Cream

1 tablespoon fresh lemon juice

1 teaspoon VegeSal

2 cups cucumbers, diced (I use the small pickling or English ones)

1 medium tomato, skinned and diced

⅛–¼ teaspoon cayenne pepper

3 tablespoons soy or almond milk

In a medium saucepan, add the water and the McKay's Chicken Style Seasoning. Heat to boiling, then add the onion. Cook on medium-low heat until onions are clear. Remove and pour into a large mixing bowl. Add the remaining ingredients, except pita pockets, and stir to combine. Place in a large food processor and process until coarsely blended. If you have a smaller food processor, then process in several small batches.

When coarsely blended, shape into 2-tablespoon-sized patties and place on a baking sheet that has been sprayed with nonstick cooking spray. Spray the tops with the nonstick cooking spray and place in a 375-degree oven for 15 minutes. Remove from oven, turn the patties over, and bake another 10 minutes. Remove and serve warm in mini pita pockets with Cucumber Sauce, lettuce, and slice of tomato, or let cool and refrigerate or freeze until ready to use.

For Cucumber Sauce: Add all ingredients to a medium-sized bowl and stir together until thoroughly mixed. Add a little more milk if needed for the desired consistency. Refrigerate until ready to serve.

These are wonderful to serve for a quick appetizer or on a buffet because you can make the patties ahead of time and then just pull them out of the refrigerator or freezer when ready to serve. You can have a whole tray of these made up in no time at all. If you can't find the mini pita pockets, you could serve these on small buns or make mini open faced sliders. —Cinda

Yield: 48 sliders; 14 ¼-cup servings cucumber sauce

(1 slider) Calories 80 Total Fat 1g Saturated Fat 0g Sodium 200mg Total Carbohydrates 14g Fiber 3g Protein 4g
(¼ cup sauce) Calories 80 Total Fat 4.5g Saturated Fat 0g Sodium 240mg Total Carbohydrates 9g Fiber 0g Protein <1g

Itty Bitty Corn Cakes

Mix flaxseed with the water and set aside for at least 5 minutes to gel. Spray a large skillet with nonstick cooking spray and sauté the **Gardenburger Veggie Medley**® Veggie Burgers until both sides are golden brown. Remove from heat and let cool slightly. When cool, place in a food processor and process until coarsely ground. Combine with the remaining ingredients in a large bowl including the gelled flaxseed. Stir to thoroughly combine.

Spray a mini muffin/tart pan with nonstick cooking spray and place a generous tablespoon of mixture into each muffin cup. Press down slightly with your fingers. Bake at 375 degrees for 15 minutes or until lightly browned. Remove from oven and take the corn cakes out of the muffin tin. Place them on a cooling rack for about 3 to 5 minutes, or until cool enough to eat. Serve warm or at room temperature.

These are great as a tasty addition to your lunch box or picnic. I like them without anything on them, but you could garnish them with all kinds of toppings. Vegan sour cream and a roasted pepper or fresh herbs would be nice, as well as some homemade salsa. If you are making them for your lunch, you could use the regular-sized muffin tin. They are so good that my guests had a hard time just eating one or two! —Cinda

1 tablespoon ground flaxseed

2 ½ tablespoons water

1 10-ounce package *Gardenburger Veggie Medley*® Veggie Burgers

1½ cups corn, frozen or fresh cut off the cob

½ cup whole-wheat flour

½ cup yellow cornmeal

2 tablespoons canned or fresh jalapeños, diced (adjust to your taste)

2 teaspoons sugar (or sweetener of your choice)

1 tablespoon cornstarch

½ teaspoon salt

½ teaspoon garlic powder

Yield: 30 mini corn cakes

(1 cake) Calories 40 Total Fat 0.5g Saturated Fat 0g Sodium 100mg Total Carbohydrates 8g Fiber 1g Protein 2g

Lil' Skillet Griddle Cakes

Cakes:

1 tablespoon grapeseed or olive oil

1 medium onion, finely diced

2 cups frozen whole kernel corn

½ cup white whole-wheat flour

½ cup yellow cornmeal

½ teaspoon sea salt

2 teaspoons baking powder

2 tablespoons cornstarch

2 teaspoons sugar

1¼ cups unsweetened original almond milk

2 tablespoons jalapeños, canned or fresh, diced (optional)

Topping:

½ cup onion, finely diced

1½ cups *Loma Linda® Redi-Burger™*

¼ teaspoon garlic powder

⅛ teaspoon ground cumin

¼ teaspoon dried oregano

Avocado Aioli:

½ cup Reduced Fat Vegenaise

1 medium avocado, remove skin and seed

For Cakes: Spray a large skillet generously with nonstick cooking spray and sauté the onion and corn together over medium-high heat. Stir often and spray again with the nonstick cooking spray if it begins to stick. Sauté until the onion is clear and the corn is golden brown. Remove from heat and set aside.

In a large mixing bowl, mix the dry ingredients together and then add the remaining ingredients, including ½ cup of the sautéed corn and onions. (Save ½ cup to use for topping.) Stir to mix well. Spray a large skillet generously with nonstick cooking spray and add 1 tablespoon of the mixture to the hot skillet, shaping into a small circle. Cook until both sides are golden brown. Remove and place on a wire rack until ready to serve. Continue with the remaining batter.

For Topping: Spray a large skillet generously with a nonstick cooking spray. Add the onion, spices, and *Loma Linda® Redi-Burger™*. Sauté until onions are clear and the *Loma Linda® Redi-Burger™* is lightly browned. Place 1 teaspoon of the mixture on each of the griddle cakes and drizzle with avocado aioli, then sprinkle with the reserved corn.

For Avocado Aioli: In a small bowl, mash avocado and mix thoroughly with the Vegenaise.

All my taste testers fell in love with this recipe! There are lots of different toppings you can add if you are feeling creative, such as sliced grape tomatoes, sliced olives, diced fresh jalapeños, or sliced green onions. The possibilities are endless! The griddle cakes freeze well, so you can make a double batch ahead of time and keep them frozen until you are ready to use them. —Cinda

Yield: 28 griddle cakes; 16 tablespoons aioli

(1 cake) Calories 80 Total Fat 3.5g Saturated Fat 0g Sodium 180mg Total Carbohydrates 9g Fiber 2g Protein 3g

(1 tablespoon aioli) Calories 45 Total Fat 4.5g Saturated Fat 0g Sodium 45mg Total Carbohydrates 2g Fiber <1g Protein 0g

Chipotle Meatballs

For Meatballs: Combine all ingredients in a medium bowl and mix well. Form into 1-inch balls. Place on a baking sheet that has been sprayed with nonstick cooking spray. Spray tops of meatballs.

Bake at 400 degrees for 15 minutes. Turn, spray with nonstick cooking spray, and bake for an additional 15 minutes.

For Spicy Chili Sauce: Puree diced tomatoes in a food processor until smooth. Sauté onion over medium-high heat in a medium-sized skillet that has been sprayed with nonstick cooking spray until clear. Add remaining ingredients. Mix well, then simmer on low for 20 minutes.

Gardenburger® Black Bean Chipotle Veggie Burgers have an amazing blend of flavors, and the chipotle in this burger really adds to the success of this dish. I also love using farro in this recipe, which is one of the healthiest grains to eat. If you don't have any on hand, you can easily substitute with cooked brown rice, but if you've never tried farro, I highly recommend it. —Brenda

Meatballs:

1 cup cooked lentils

1 cup cooked farro

1 10-ounce package *Gardenburger®* Black Bean Chipotle Veggie Burgers

⅛ teaspoon cayenne pepper

1 medium onion, pureed in 2 tablespoons water

½ cup pecans, chopped fine

1 cup quick oats

Spicy Chili Sauce:

1 14.5-ounce can petite diced tomatoes

¼ cup onion, finely diced

1 cup ketchup

3 tablespoons brown sugar

2 tablespoons vegetarian Worcestershire sauce

2 teaspoons Bragg Liquid Aminos

2 tablespoons fresh lemon juice

4 teaspoons double concentrated tomato paste

1 teaspoon red pepper flakes

2 teaspoons original Cholula sauce

Yield: 54 1-inch meatballs and sauce

(1 meatball and sauce) Calories 40 Total Fat 1g Saturated Fat 0g Sodium 80mg Total Carbohydrates 7g Fiber 1g Protein 1g

Fiesta Cornballs

3 cups water

2 teaspoons salt

½ teaspoon dried thyme

½ teaspoon dried oregano

1¾ cups ground cornmeal

2 tablespoons jalapeños, canned or fresh, chopped

2 cups frozen corn

1 cup *Loma Linda® Redi-Burger™*

In a medium saucepan, bring the water to a boil and add the salt and spices, then slowly pour in the cornmeal, stirring constantly. Stir constantly until thickened, approximately 2 minutes. Remove from heat and add the remaining ingredients. Mix well.

Form into 1-tablespoon-sized balls and place on a baking sheet that has been sprayed with nonstick cooking spray. Refrigerate for at least 30 minutes. When ready to bake, place them in a preheated oven at 400 degrees and bake for 30 minutes, or until golden brown and firm. Serve warm with your favorite marinara sauce.

This recipe combines two of my favorite things—polenta and spicy hot things! Which makes these little appetizers absolutely amazing. I actually add more jalapeños to mine, but you can add as little or as much as your taste buds prefer. They freeze well, so you can make them ahead of time and just pull them out of the freezer and warm up. —Cinda

Yield: 60 cornballs

(1 cornball) Calories 30 Total Fat 0g Saturated Fat 0g Sodium 125mg Total Carbohydrates 4g Fiber <1g Protein 2g

Salads and Sandwiches

Thai Cole Slaw
p. 64

Ranch Hand Salad
p. 62

Black Bean
Burger Pockets p. 70

Polish Potato Salad
p. 60

Cholula Burger
p. 69

Bangkok Barbecue
p. 76

Polish Potato Salad

8 medium potatoes, peeled and halved

1 20-ounce can *Loma Linda* Big Franks, sliced

1 teaspoon red pepper flakes

3 cups sauerkraut

2 tablespoons soy margarine

¼ cup Wondra flour

1 cup unsweetened almond milk

½ cup original Silk creamer

½ teaspoon onion powder

½ teaspoon parsley

1 teaspoon salt (or to taste)

Boil potatoes until tender (but not mushy). Drain and cut into thick, round slices. Place in a large bowl with the *Loma Linda* Big Franks, red pepper flakes, and sauerkraut.

Melt margarine in a saucepan over medium heat. Add Wondra flour and blend with a fork or wire whisk. Add milk and whisk together until smooth. Add Silk creamer, onion powder, parsley, and salt. Cook until thickened, and then pour over potatoes. Mix well. Serve hot.

When I think of Polish cuisine, I almost always associate it with some sort of dish that consists of potatoes and sauerkraut—and I just happen to love both! My grandparents were from Eastern Europe, so many of our family recipes that have been passed down have Polish influence. This potato salad has both of these favorite ingredients, and instead of serving cold as are typical potato salads, this dish is served hot! But honestly, I love it both hot and cold! Why not try both and discover your own favorite? —Brenda

Yield: 18 ½-cup servings

(½ cup) Calories 120 Total Fat 2.5g Saturated Fat 0g Sodium 340mg Total Carbohydrates 18g Fiber 3g Protein 7g

Sweet Potato Salad

Place cubed sweet potatoes in a large saucepan. Cover with water and add salt. Bring to a boil over medium-high heat, then turn down and simmer for 15 minutes or until tender. Drain. Place in a medium-sized bowl.

Combine **Worthington® Vegetable Skallops®** and cinnamon. Sauté over medium-high heat in a skillet that has been sprayed with nonstick cooking spray, until golden brown.

Add **Worthington® Vegetable Skallops®** and remaining ingredients, including prepared dressing to a medium-sized bowl and mix well. Serve over lettuce.

For Dressing: Combine all ingredients in a small bowl. Mix well.

This recipe is similar to a dish I had at a church potluck in Hawaii. I liked it so much, I went home and tried to recreate it. This definitely has an "island influence" and is pretty close to what I had originally. Sometimes when I'm in a hurry, instead of boiling, I cook the sweet potatoes in the microwave and it works just as well. This is also a great recipe when you have leftover baked sweet potatoes. —Brenda

3 cups sweet potatoes, peeled and cubed

1 teaspoon salt

1 cup *Worthington® Vegetable Skallops®*, diced

¼ teaspoon cinnamon

1 cup mandarin oranges

1 medium apple, peeled and chopped

½ cup pecan halves, toasted in skillet

¼ cup dried cranberries

Dressing:

2 tablespoons orange juice

1 tablespoon agave nectar

½ cup Grapeseed Vegenaise

⅛ teaspoon salt

¼ teaspoon ginger

½ teaspoon cinnamon

Yield: 12 ½-cup servings

(½ cup) Calories 160 Total Fat 9g Saturated Fat 1g Sodium 360mg Total Carbohydrates 15g Fiber 2g Protein 4g

Ranch Hand Salad

1 19-ounce can *Loma Linda* Tender Bits

2 cups corn chips, crushed

8 cups romaine lettuce, rinsed and torn into bite-sized pieces

4 cups fresh corn, roasted and cut off the cob

2 cups canned black beans, rinsed and drained

Grape tomatoes

Black olives

Sliced pickled jalapeños, optional

Smoky Barbecue Vinaigrette:

⅓ cup smoky barbecue sauce

¼ cup extra virgin olive oil

1 tablespoon honey

2 tablespoons fresh lemon juice

Salt to taste

Avocado Ranch Dressing:

½ cup Grapeseed Vegenaise

3 tablespoons original soymilk or almond milk

¼ teaspoon onion salt

¼ teaspoon garlic powder

⅛ teaspoon garlic salt

½ teaspoon dried marjoram

1 teaspoon dried parsley

1 medium ripe avocado

Dip each of the *Loma Linda* Tender Bits into the crushed corn chips until well coated. Place on a baking sheet that has been sprayed with nonstick cooking spray. Spray the tops of the coated *Loma Linda* Tender Bits with the nonstick cooking spray and place in a 375-degree oven for 15 minutes. Remove from oven and turn each of the *Loma Linda* Tender Bits over. Return to oven for another 15 minutes or until golden brown and crispy. Remove from oven and set aside.

To assemble salad, place 1 cup of romaine lettuce on each of 8 individual salad plates. Sprinkle ½ cup of corn over the top and then ¼ cup of the black beans. Add as many tomatoes and black olives as you would like and also the pickled jalapeño slices. Place the baked *Loma Linda* Tender Bits pieces around the edge, dividing them equally between the 8 individual salad plates. Drizzle the Smoky Barbecue Vinaigrette and the Avocado Ranch Dressing over the top of each salad. Serve immediately.

For Smoky Barbecue Vinaigrette: In a small shaker or bowl, mix all ingredients until well blended.

For Avocado Ranch Dressing: Peel and remove the seed from the avocado. Mash the avocado with a fork in a small bowl until mushy. Add the remaining ingredients and stir until well blended, adding more almond milk or soymilk if needed. Refrigerate until ready to use.

Don't let the length of ingredients, or instructions of this recipe scare you off! It is worth every bit of effort! Actually, it is a lot easier than it looks. The two dressings can be made a couple days ahead of time, and the same goes with the roasted corn. If you don't have fresh corn on the cob to roast, you can use frozen corn and toast it in a skillet on the stove until a golden and even a little charred. Serve buffet style and let the guests assemble their own salads. —Cinda

Yield: 8 salads, 10 tablespoons Smoky Barbecue Vinaigrette, 20 tablespoons Avocado Ranch Dressing

(1 salad) Calories 270 Total Fat 4g Saturated Fat 0.5g Sodium 580mg Total Carbohydrates 47g Fiber 8g Protein 15g

(1 tablespoon vinaigrette) Calories 70 Total Fat 5g Saturated Fat 0.5g Sodium 10mg Total Carbohydrates 5g Fiber <1g Protein <1g

(1 tablespoon dressing) Calories 50 Total Fat 5g Saturated Fat 0.5g Sodium 80mg Total Carbohydrates <1g Fiber <1g Protein <1g

Eight Layer Taco Salad

Mix the hot rice and salsa together to make Spanish rice. Spray a skillet with nonstick cooking spray and sauté the crumbled *MorningStar Farms*® Roasted Garlic and Quinoa Burgers over medium-high heat till hot and slightly browned. On 8 plates, layer the following ingredients evenly:

- Tortilla chips
- Spanish rice
- Refried beans
- Vegan cheese
- Crumbled burger
- Lettuce
- Tomatoes
- Olives

Garnish with avocados, Tofutti Better Than Sour Cream, chives, and salsa.

This eight-layer taco salad reminds us of haystacks, and who doesn't love haystacks? This is one of those quick and easy meals that are so delicious! Try adding sautéed onions or hot banana peppers. This is a meal all by itself and is one of our family favorites! —Linda

2 cups hot cooked brown rice

½ cup salsa

2 cups *MorningStar Farms*® Roasted Garlic and Quinoa Burgers, crumbled

2 cups fresh tomatoes, diced

2 cups romaine lettuce, shredded

1 cup olives, sliced

2 cups hot refried beans

1 cup vegan cheese, grated

4 cups baked tortilla chips

Avocados

Tofutti Better Than Sour Cream

Chives

Salsa

Yield: 8 2-cup salads

(1 salad) Calories 290 Total Fat 9g Saturated Fat 2g Sodium 950mg Total Carbohydrates 44g Fiber 9g Protein 10g

Thai Cole Slaw

1 cup *Worthington® Vegetable Skallops®*, diced

1 tablespoon jalapeño nacho slices, diced

Salt to taste

2 cups carrots, shredded

4 cups cabbage, shredded

2 cups pea pods, sliced at angles in thirds

1 cup peanuts, chopped

Dressing:

2 cloves fresh garlic

1 tablespoon jalapeño nacho slices

⅓ cup cilantro, chopped

¼ cup fresh lime juice

1 tablespoon Bragg Liquid Aminos

1 tablespoon agave nectar

1½ teaspoons sesame oil

¼ teaspoon salt

In a skillet that has been sprayed with nonstick cooking spray, combine *Worthington® Vegetable Skallops®*, diced jalapeños, and salt and sauté over medium-high heat until *Worthington® Vegetable Skallops®* are golden brown. Remove from heat and cool completely.

Place carrots, cabbage, pea pods, and peanuts in a medium-sized bowl. Mix well.

Add cooled *Worthington® Vegetable Skallops®* to vegetables and pour dressing over the top. Mix well. Garnish with extra chopped peanuts.

For Dressing: In blender or food processor, combine garlic, jalapeño pepper, cilantro, lime juice, Bragg Liquid Aminos, agave nectar, sesame oil, and salt. Process until smooth, stopping occasionally to scrape sides of processor.

I love Thai food especially the freshness in their vegetables and spices. This salad is one of my all time favorites. In my opinion the jalapeños really make this dish come alive. Normally I wouldn't think of jalapeños in Thai food, but my favorite Thai restaurant changed my mind. I was amazed at how many dishes showcased my favorite pepper! That was all I needed for inspiration for this recipe . . . and thus Thai Cole Slaw was created! —Brenda

Yield: 18 ½-cup servings

(½ cup) Calories 90 Total Fat 5g Saturated Fat 1g Sodium 230mg Total Carbohydrates 6g Fiber 2g Protein 7g

Chicken Asparagus Salad

Cut the **Worthington® Vegetable Skallops®** into strips and place them in a skillet that has been sprayed with nonstick cooking spray over medium-high heat. Sauté until they are golden brown. Remove from heat and cool slightly.

Tear the lettuce into bite-size pieces and place on a platter. Sprinkle the grated carrot on top of lettuce. Place the tomato wedges on the lettuce and carrot and add the **Worthington® Vegetable Skallops®** and asparagus. Drizzle the spicy ranch dressing on top or serve on the side.

For Spicy Ranch Dressing: In a small bowl, mix all ingredients together and chill in the refrigerator.

*I love **Worthington® Vegetable Skallops®** because you can use them in just about any recipe that calls for chicken. This product does not have a strong flavor, so it takes on all the spices and seasonings in the recipe. It is also has a nice chewy texture, so it can be used in many different kinds of recipes. Add your favorite raw veggies to this salad to make it even better. Instead of asparagus try using fresh steamed broccoli—but don't over cook it, keep it "tender crunchy." You can serve in one large bowl or on individual plates. —Linda*

1 cup **Worthington® Vegetable Skallops®**

2 cups leafy green lettuce

¼ cup carrots, grated

½ cup fresh tomato, cut into wedges

½ cup asparagus, lightly steamed

Spicy Ranch Dressing:

¼ cup Reduced Fat Vegenaise

½ teaspoon ketchup

Dash cayenne pepper

⅛ teaspoon red pepper flakes

Dash seasoned salt

Yield: 4 salads

(1 salad) Calories 110 Total Fat 6g Saturated Fat 0g Sodium 300mg Total Carbohydrates 6g Fiber 3g Protein 9g

Redi Sandwich Spread

1 19-ounce can *Loma Linda® Redi-Burger*™

¼ cup dill pickle relish

½ cup Grapeseed Vegenaise

¼ cup Tofutti Better Than Sour Cream

¼ cup red pepper, chopped fine

¼ cup yellow pepper, chopped fine

¼ cup black olives, sliced

Crumble the **Loma Linda® Redi-Burger**™ into small shreds. Add the remaining ingredients and stir until it is well mixed. Refrigerate until chilled. Serve cold with homemade bread, oven fries, and a fresh fruit salad.

This easy sandwich filling can also be made into an oven open-faced meal. Just mix the spread with ½ cup of vegan cheese and spread on half of a bun. Put the open faced sandwiches under the broiler for 1 to 2 minutes or until cheese is melted. Serve with fresh fruit and a favorite dessert. —Linda

Yield: 14 ¼-cup servings

(¼ cup) Calories 120 Total Fat 7g Saturated Fat 1g Sodium 330mg Total Carbohydrates 6g Fiber 2g Protein 8g

Home Run Sandwich

In a medium bowl, mash the **Loma Linda**® Big Franks with a fork or potato masher until it looks like small to medium crumbles. In a small bowl, mix the Vegenaise, Sriracha, and pickle relish. Add the **Loma Linda**® Big Franks and mix well. Spread ½ cup onto each of 4 bread slices, then top with another slice. Cut in half.

I love the sweet and spicy surprise your taste buds get when you bite into this sandwich! You can add more of the Sriracha hot sauce if you like things even spicier like my husband Joel does. You can also add some chopped celery to it for a little crunch. —Cinda

- 1 20-ounce can **Loma Linda**® Big Franks
- ½ cup Reduced Fat Vegenaise
- 1½ tablespoons Sriracha (or your favorite hot sauce)
- 4 tablespoons sweet pickle relish
- 8 slices whole-wheat bread

Yield: 8 ½ sandwiches

(½ sandwich) Calories 190 Total Fat 8g Saturated Fat 0g Sodium 610mg Total Carbohydrates 18g Fiber 6g Protein 14g

Choplet Burger

1 cup onion, slivered

2 cups fresh mushrooms, sliced

¼ teaspoon salt

1 tablespoon water

1 20-ounce can *Worthington® Choplets®*

8 slices fresh tomato

8 slices vegan cheese

8 leaves green leafy lettuce

8 whole-wheat hamburger buns

Seasoned Breading Mix:

½ cup unbleached all-purpose flour

1 teaspoon McKay's Chicken Style Seasoning

½ teaspoon McKay's Beef Style Seasoning

¼ cup nutritional yeast flakes

½ teaspoon onion powder

⅛ teaspoon garlic powder

Thousand Island Dressing:

¼ cup Grapeseed Vegenaise

1 tablespoon ketchup

2 teaspoons dill pickle relish

Place the onions and mushrooms in a glass dish in the microwave with the salt and water. Cook for 3 to 4 minutes or until tender. Set aside.

Spray a large skillet with nonstick cooking spray and heat over medium high. Dip the *Worthington® Choplets®* in the prepared seasoned breading mix and cook on both sides in the skillet until the *Worthington® Choplets®* are golden brown. Lay a piece of vegan cheese on each *Worthington® Choplets®* and continue to cook until the cheese is melted. Spread the buns with 2 teaspoons Thousand Island Dressing per burger. Place the onions, mushrooms, and lettuce on top of the *Worthington® Choplets®* and cheese. Serve hot.

For Breading Mix: Combine all ingredients in a small bowl.

For Thousand Island Dressing: Mix all ingredients together in a small bowl and refrigerate until ready to use.

Worthington® Choplets® have always been a favorite in the Micheff household! Mom would serve them as sandwiches or fry them and put them in a casserole dish with gravy on top and bake it. And we all loved them! Now that I have a home of my own I serve Worthington® Choplets® to my family, and they love them too! I like to serve these Worthington® Choplets® Burgers with baked beans, potato salad, and homemade cookies. It is also good with sautéed sweet red peppers. —Linda

Yield: 8 burgers

(1 burger) Calories 340 Total Fat 13g Saturated Fat 4g Sodium 910mg Total Carbohydrates 36g Fiber 6g Protein 17g

Cholula Burger

Mix the flour and nutritional yeast flakes in a small wide bowl, and stir to combine. Coat each side of the **Worthington® Choplets®** in the flour mixture until well coated. (You can dip them in the juice from the can and dip them again in the flour mixture to thoroughly coat them.) Place **Worthington® Choplets®** on a baking sheet that has been sprayed with nonstick cooking spray. Spray the top of each of the **Worthington® Choplets®** with the nonstick cooking spray and place in a 350-degree oven for 15 minutes. Turn them over and spray again with the nonstick cooking spray. Return to the oven and bake another 15 minutes.

In a glass pie plate or microwaveable dish, place the slivered onions and melted vegan margarine. Microwave on high for approximately 10 minutes or until onions are clear and slightly browned. Remove and set aside.

In a small bowl, mix together the Cholula and Vegenaise. Spread each sandwich bun with the sauce, dividing equally between the halves. Place a piece of lettuce and two warm **Worthington® Choplets®** on the bottom slice of bread and then top with the tomato slices, avocado slices, pickled jalapeños, and the slivered onions. Serve warm.

Our mom use to make us Choplet® sandwiches when we were kids and I still love them to this day. However, my version of this childhood favorite has gotten a little more sophisticated from the ones we grew up eating. If you don't like things quite as spicy as I do, you can leave off the pickled jalapeños. You can also add your own favorite hot sauce if you cannot find the Cholula brand. —Cinda

1 cup whole-wheat flour

¾ cup nutritional yeast flakes

4 *Worthington® Choplets®*

1 large onion, slivered

1 tablespoon soy margarine, melted

2 teaspoons original Cholula hot sauce

2 tablespoons Reduced Fat Vegenaise

Sliced avocado

Pickled jalapeño slices

Lettuce

Sliced tomatoes

2 whole-wheat sandwich buns

Yield: 4 ½ sandwiches

(½ sandwich) Calories 150 Total Fat 5g Saturated Fat 0.5g Sodium 440mg Total Carbohydrates 17g Fiber 4g Protein 11g

Black Bean Burger Pockets

1 cup onions, slivered

¼ teaspoon red pepper flakes

¼ teaspoon salt

1 10-ounce package *Gardenburger*®
Black Bean Chipotle Veggie
Burgers, cut in medium pieces

1⅓ cups canned garbanzo beans

1 cup fresh spinach, chopped

½ cup salsa

1 cup fresh tomatoes, chopped

½ cup olives, sliced

½ cup Tofutti Better Than Sour
Cream

8 slices avocado

4 slices pita bread, halved

Sauté the onion slivers in a skillet that has been sprayed with nonstick cooking spray and heat over medium high. Add the salt and red pepper flakes and continue sautéing until the onions are clear. Add the *Gardenburger*® Black Bean Chipotle Veggie Burgers and garbanzo beans and sauté for another 5 to 10 minutes. Remove from heat and add the spinach.

Fill each halved pita bread with ½ cup of burger mixture and add 1 tablespoon of salsa on top. Then add the chopped tomatoes, olives, and Tofutti Better Than Sour Cream. Top with an avocado slice.

This is a quick meal that is very nutritious and tasty too! It also is so filling! It does have a bit of a spicy flavor, so if you are one that does not like the extra spicy taste, then just leave out the red pepper flakes.
—Linda

Yield: 8 ½ pitas

(½ pita) Calories 250 Total Fat 10g Saturated Fat 1g Sodium 680mg Total Carbohydrates 35g Fiber 6g Protein 8g

Triple Bean Burgers

Place onion in a shallow microwaveable dish. Mix the McKay's Chicken Style Seasoning with the water and pour over the onions. Microwave for approximately 10 minutes or until onion is clear. Set aside.

Mix all of the beans in a large bowl. In small batches, place them in a food processor and process until they are mostly mashed with only a few pieces of the beans remaining, adding a little water to the blender if necessary. Place in a large bowl and add the remaining ingredients. Stir to thoroughly mix. Using a ½ cup measuring cup, form into round patties. Place on a baking sheet that has been sprayed with a nonstick cooking spray. Spray the tops of the patties with the nonstick cooking spray before placing in a 375-degree oven for 20 minutes. Remove from oven and turn patties over. Spray again with the nonstick cooking spray and return to the oven for another 15 to 20 minutes or until golden brown and crispy on the outside. Remove from oven and serve warm in a whole-wheat bun. These burgers freeze well.

I have always been told that I take after my dad, and I am sure that is where I get my love for sandwiches! I particularly like veggie burgers, and have created many different kinds over the years. This recipe is packed with nutrition and flavor. It is easy to make, and you can double the recipe so you have more to freeze. I just pop one in the toaster when I want a quick meal. The toaster not only heats it up, but it makes it crispy too. I also add chopped jalapeños to mine for a little spice. —Cinda

Ingredients

- 1 medium onion, finely diced
- ½ cup water
- 1 teaspoon McKay's Chicken Style Seasoning
- 1 15-ounce can black beans, drained
- 1 16-ounce can garbanzo beans, drained
- 1 16-ounce can dark red kidney beans, drained
- 2 cups cooked short grain brown rice
- 1 cup fresh carrot, grated
- 1½ cups walnuts, finely ground
- 1¾ cups fresh or dried bread crumbs
- 2 tablespoons ground flax seeds
- 2 tablespoons Bragg Liquid Aminos
- 3 tablespoons nutritional yeast flakes
- 2 teaspoons VegeSal, or an all-purpose vegetable seasoning
- 2 teaspoons Italian seasoning
- 1 19-ounce can *Loma Linda® Vege-Burger®*

Yield: 22 burgers

(1 burger) Calories 180 Total Fat 5g Saturated Fat 0.5g Sodium 590mg Total Carbohydrates 23g Fiber 4g Protein 12g

Black Bean Bistro Burgers

2 cloves fresh garlic, minced

1 large onion, diced

2 cups fresh mushrooms, diced

1 15-ounce can black beans, undrained

⅓ cup yellow pepper, diced

1 tablespoon McKay's Chicken Style Seasoning

1 teaspoon parsley flakes

¼ teaspoon ground cumin

2 cups quick oats

2 cups Pepperidge Farm Stuffing Mix or bread crumbs

½ teaspoon cayenne

¼ teaspoon dried oregano

1 tablespoon Bragg Liquid Aminos

1 tablespoon vegan Worcestershire sauce

1 9.5-ounce package *MorningStar Farms*® Roasted Garlic and Quinoa Burgers, thawed and crumbled

1 cup almond milk

Sauté garlic, onion, and mushrooms in a skillet that has been sprayed with nonstick cooking spray over medium heat until onion is clear.

In a large bowl, stir together remaining ingredients, except milk. Add sautéed vegetables. Stir in milk, let stand for 5 minutes to absorb liquid. Form into 4-inch patties and place on a baking sheet that has been sprayed with nonstick cooking spray. Spray tops of patties as well. Bake at 400 degrees for 15 minutes. Spray tops of patties before flipping. Flip and bake for an additional 15 minutes.

I made these burgers a bit bigger than usual because the store-bought buns are typically so much larger, but these burgers will fill it up just fine! If you want to make them smaller, it's not a problem. You'll just have more burgers! Fortunately, they freeze very well. I bake my burgers in an effort to keep the fat calories low, but on special occasions, I will fry them with a little canola oil. To be honest, I like the fried ones better but knowing how much healthier the baked ones are makes this recipe my favorite just the way it is! —Brenda

Yield: 10 4-inch burgers

(1 burger) Calories 210 Total Fat 5g Saturated Fat 0.5g Sodium 750mg Total Carbohydrates 36g Fiber 8g Protein 10g

Grilled Avocado Chipotle Burger

Over medium-high heat, sauté onion in a skillet that has been sprayed with a nonstick cooking spray. Continue sautéing until caramelized.

Grill *Gardenburger*® Black Bean Chipotle Veggie Burgers on both sides over medium heat in a skillet that has been sprayed with nonstick cooking spray until browned.

Drizzle 1 tablespoon jalapeño sauce on each side of a whole grain bun. Place ¼ of the avocado slices on one side, top with patty and remaining half of bun. Serve with condiments of your choice.

For Jalapeño Sauce: Combine all ingredients in a blender. Blend until smooth.

*The **Gardenburger**® Black Bean Chipotle Veggie Burgers have a wonderful combination of flavors all by themselves, but when you add the jalapeño sauce and avocado, you'll almost think you are in Mexico! All you need is a sombrero, which actually isn't a bad idea! It makes a great bowl for the tostado chips! —Brenda*

1 medium onion, slivered

1 10-ounce package *Gardenburger*® Black Bean Chipotle Veggie Burgers

8 whole-grain buns

1 medium avocado, slivered

Jalapeño Sauce:

1 tablespoon fresh cilantro

¼ cup Tofutti Better Than Sour Cream

¼ cup jalapeño nacho slices

1 tablespoon fresh jalapeño pepper, diced

1 tablespoon lemon juice

¼ teaspoon onion powder

¼ teaspoon garlic powder

¼ teaspoon dried or fresh parsley

1 teaspoon agave nectar

Pinch of salt

Yield: 4 burgers

(1 burger) Calories 300 Total Fat 12g Saturated Fat 1.5g Sodium 720mg Total Carbohydrates 44g Fiber 11g Protein 11g

European Barbecue Sandwich

1 10-ounce package *MorningStar Farms*® Hickory BBQ Riblets

1 large onion, slivered

2 cups fresh mushrooms, sliced

1–2 tablespoons canola, grapeseed, or extra virgin olive oil

8 slices European whole-wheat bread

Thaw frozen *MorningStar Farms*® Hickory BBQ Riblets on a dish. While they are thawing, sauté the onions and mushrooms in 1 to 2 tablespoons of oil in a skillet over medium-high heat until onions are clear and slightly golden.

Cut each of the thawed *MorningStar Farms*® Hickory BBQ Riblets into small strips and add them and the sauce from the *MorningStar Farms*® Hickory BBQ Riblets to the sautéed onions and mushrooms. Stir to combine and let cook over medium heat until hot and bubbly. Place ½ cup of the mixture onto each of the bread slices. Garnish as desired and serve warm.

I love to serve these on a buffet with a variety of toppings and let each person make their own. I make several batches and put them in a warming dish and place a basket of the bread slices next to it. This is also delicious over baked potatoes, so I have a bowl of them on the buffet as well. It is fun to watch everyone creating their own culinary masterpieces! —Cinda

Yield: 8 open-faced sandwiches

(1 sandwich) Calories 150 Total Fat 3.5g Saturated Fat 0g Sodium 330mg Total Carbohydrates 24g Fiber 3g Protein 8g

Santorini Barbecue

Spray a large skillet generously with a nonstick cooking spray. Sauté the onion on medium to low heat until clear and then add the remaining ingredients except the *MorningStar Farms*® Hickory BBQ Riblets. Sauté until vegetables are tender but firm. Add the Riblets and the sauce and gently stir to combine. Serve on warm whole-wheat buns.

This reminds me of some of the wonderful food we had when we were in Greece. The flavors of all the fresh vegetables cooked together taste as delicious as they smell. You could sprinkle some fresh oregano over the top for added flavor. This is also good over pasta or brown rice.
—Cinda

1 medium onion, diced

3 cloves garlic, minced

4 cups fresh mushrooms, coarsely chopped

2 cups fresh tomatoes, diced

6 cups eggplant, cubed

1½ cups zucchini, cubed

1½ cups yellow squash, cubed

½–1 teaspoon red pepper flakes

1 10-ounce package *MorningStar Farms*® Hickory BBQ Riblets, cut into small strips

Salt to taste

Yield: 12 ½-cup servings

(½ cup) Calories 60 Total Fat 1g Saturated Fat 0g Sodium 140mg Total Carbohydrates 11g Fiber 3g Protein 5g

Bangkok Barbecue

1 cup water

4 cups onions, slivered

2 cups red and yellow peppers, slivered

1 package *MorningStar Farms®* Hickory BBQ Riblets, cut into small pieces

1 teaspoon red pepper flakes (use less if desired)

½ teaspoon sea salt

¼ teaspoon seasoned salt

In a skillet on medium-high heat, place the water and onions and cook until all the water is gone. Continue sautéing until the onions turn a golden brown, stirring constantly. Add the slivered peppers and sauté for another 5 minutes. Add the remaining ingredients and mix well.

Bangkok Barbecue was a real hit with my family! To give it more zip, add a hot pepper to the red and yellow peppers. This barbecue is great at church fellowship meals, birthday parties, and just a family meal at home! Serve this barbecue with homemade hamburger buns and Grapeseed Vegenaise, a fresh fruit salad, and a favorite dessert.
—Linda

Yield: 8 1-cup servings

(1 cup) Calories 90 Total Fat 1g Saturated Fat 0g Sodium 430mg Total Carbohydrates 16g Fiber 4g Protein 6g

Avocado Chicken Salad Sandwiches

Rinse and drain the chickpeas. Place on a paper towel and remove the outer skins. Process the beans and the *MorningStar Farms® Grillers®* Chik'n Veggie Patties in a food processor until fine. In a medium bowl, using a fork or potato masher, mash the avocado. Add the remaining ingredients and mix well. Spread mixture on bread and top with your favorite sandwich toppings.

This sandwich spread also makes a great dip. Try serving with cut up veggies, crackers, or pita chips. Surprisingly enough, you can make this up ahead of time and keep in your refrigerator. When I created this recipe, I wanted to just test it to see how long it would keep in the refrigerator before it turned dark. Usually avocados turn dark the next day, so I wasn't very hopeful. But to my surprise, it stayed a beautiful shade of green for an entire week! Of course, I don't recommend eating it after this long, but it was nice to know that it retained such a beautiful green color! —Brenda

1 9.5-ounce package *MorningStar Farms® Grillers®* Chik'n Veggie Patties

1 15-ounce can garbanzo beans

1 large ripe avocado

¼ cup jalapeño nacho slices, diced

2 tablespoons fresh lime juice

½ teaspoon salt

Yield: 6 ¼-cup servings

(¼ cup) Calories 130 Total Fat 7g Saturated Fat 1g Sodium 450mg Total Carbohydrates 14g Fiber 3g Protein 5g

Sloppy Joes

3 10-ounce packages *Gardenburger Veggie Medley*® Veggie Burgers

1 medium onion, chopped

1 15-ounce can tomato sauce

⅛ teaspoon cayenne pepper

¼ teaspoon red pepper flakes

2 cups ketchup

¼ cup brown sugar

½ cup fresh lemon juice

2 tablespoons vegetarian Worcestershire sauce

1 teaspoon chili powder

16 whole-wheat buns

Crumble *Gardenburger Veggie Medley*® Veggie Burgers in a skillet that has been sprayed with nonstick cooking spray. Sauté over medium heat until browned. In a separate skillet that has been sprayed with nonstick cooking spray, sauté onions over medium-high heat until clear. Add remaining ingredients, including burger, and stir well. Simmer for 15 to 20 minutes and serve hot on whole-wheat buns.

Some people think a burger is only to be eaten on a bun, but there's so many different ways to use this wonderful product. The Gardenburger Veggie Medley® Veggie Burgers crumble easily to become more of a "hamburger" consistency, and the recipe ideas are endless. I've used this product in spaghetti sauce and it's wonderful! You can substitute it for just about any recipe that calls for hamburger! My husband, Tim, loves Sloppy Joes but doesn't like the mess, so if you feel the same way, just serve them open face on a plate and eat with a fork! For those who love the traditional experience, be sure and have lots of napkins on hand! —Brenda

Yield: 16 ½-cup sandwiches

(1 sandwich) Calories 220 Total Fat 4g Saturated Fat 0.5g Sodium 620mg Total Carbohydrates 46g Fiber 7g Protein 7g

Hawaiian Hot Pockets

In a large skillet, place the water, olive oil, and McKay's Chicken Style Seasoning. Bring to a boil and add the onion and celery. Let sauté over medium heat, stirring often, until onion is clear. Add the *MorningStar Farms® Grillers®* Chik'n Veggie Patties, the peppers, and the pineapple (the juice will be used in the sauce) and continue to sauté, making sure to stir often until a little browned. Add the thickened sauce and stir to mix well.

Open the crescent rolls and separate the dough from each can into 4 squares (2 triangles per square). Place ⅓ cup of the filling in the middle of each square and fold each corner into the middle. Pinch the very top to seal. You do not have to seal the other seams unless you prefer to. Place on a baking sheet that has been sprayed with a nonstick cooking spray and bake in a 350-degree oven for 12 to 14 minutes or until golden brown. Let cool for at least 5 minutes before eating.

For Sauce: Place all of the ingredients in a small saucepan. Bring to a boil, then reduce heat to low and let simmer for approximately 15 minutes or until thickened. Stir occasionally. When thickened, remove from heat.

I love pretty much any kind of sandwich—guess you can say that I take after my dad! That is also where I get my love for anything spicy! This recipe is definitely a winner because first of all, it is a sandwich . . . and second . . . it is spicy! But not too spicy and with just a hint of sweet. You could also use homemade bread dough in place of the Crescent dough if you have the time to make it. Since these can be eaten at room temperature, they are great to take on a picnic or in your lunch. —Cinda

¼ cup water

1 tablespoon extra virgin olive oil

1 tablespoon McKay's Chicken Style Seasoning

1 medium onion, diced fine

1 cup celery, diced

1 9.5-ounce package *MorningStar Farms® Grillers®* Chik'n Veggie Patties, cut into small thin strips

1 cup red, yellow, and orange bell peppers, diced

1 8-ounce can crushed pineapple, drained (reserve the juice)

2 8-ounce cans Low-Fat Pillsbury Crescent Rolls

Sauce:

½ cup apricot jam

1 tablespoon fresh lemon juice

½ teaspoon cayenne pepper

⅛ teaspoon salt

Reserved pineapple juice

Yield: 16 ½-hot pocket sandwiches

(½ hot pocket) Calories 160 Total Fat 6g Saturated Fat 2g Sodium 410mg Total Carbohydrates 24g Fiber 2g Protein 5g

Zesty Chili Burritos

½ cup water

1 cup onion, diced fine

1 teaspoon onion powder

½ teaspoon sea salt

½ teaspoon seasoned salt

1 teaspoon red pepper flakes

1 20-ounce can *Worthington* Chili

1 cup diced canned tomatoes (can use fresh)

2 cups cooked brown rice

8 8-inch flour tortillas

½ cup Tofutti Better Than Sour Cream

½ cup olives, sliced (optional)

1 cup fresh tomatoes, diced (optional)

In a large skillet on medium-high heat, place the water and onions and cook until water is evaporated. Add the seasonings, *Worthington* Chili, tomatoes, and rice and simmer for approximately 15 to 20 minutes. Remove from heat and add ½ cup of filling to each tortilla. Add the diced tomatoes and olives, then top with Tofutti Better Than Sour Cream. Roll up like a burrito. Serve hot.

These Zesty Chili Burritos were an instant hit with my family! I used the canned **Worthington** *Chili, which took the work right out of the meal! For the rice I like to cook up a big pot of brown rice and keep it in my refrigerator. It makes this quick and easy meal even faster!* —Linda

Yield: 8 burritos

(1 burrito) Calories 340 Total Fat 7g Saturated Fat 0.5g Sodium 1080mg Total Carbohydrates 56g Fiber 8g Protein 15g

Soups and Stews

Chicken Noodle Soup
p. 85

Tijuana Minestrone
p. 90

Steakhouse Stew
p. 100

Sweet Potato Chili
p. 103

Split Pea Soup
p. 95

Seaside Chowder
p. 94

Asian Vegetable Soup

8 cups water

2 cups dried Shiitake mushrooms, broken into medium size pieces

6 tablespoons oriental vegetable seasoning

1 cup celery, diced

2 cups carrots, cut into thin rounds

2 cups fresh broccoli florets

2 cups snow peas, cut in half

2 cups *Loma Linda*® Tender Bits, coarsely diced

In a large stockpot, place the water and the dried Shiitake mushrooms. Bring to a boil and then reduce heat and cook for 25 minutes at a low boil. Add the seasoning and stir to mix well. Add all of the vegetables and *Loma Linda*® Tender Bits, then remove from heat. Let sit for 4 minutes and serve in bowls with brown rice.

My brother, Ken, who is an excellent cook, taught me how to make this soup. He used different vegetables when he made it for my husband, Joel, and I, but he said that he makes it different every time he makes it! You just put in whatever vegetables that you have a taste for . . . or have on hand! I love that it is low in calories and high in nutrition, not to mention, super easy to make. —Cinda

Yield: 12 1-cup servings

(1 cup) Calories 60 Total Fat 1g Saturated Fat 0g Sodium 940mg Total Carbohydrates 7g Fiber 2g Protein 4g

Chicken Noodle Soup

In a stockpot that has been sprayed with nonstick cooking spray, sauté onions over medium heat until clear. Add water, McKay's Chicken Style Seasoning, Better Than Bouillon No-Chicken Base, parsley, carrots, celery, **Loma Linda**® Tender Bits, and barley. Simmer until carrots are tender, approximately 15 minutes. Add potatoes and simmer for another 10 minutes or until tender. Add noodles and cook an additional 10 minutes or until pasta is al dente.

*My grandsons love **Loma Linda**® Tender Bits, so when I added them to the soup, they had one more reason to love it! This soup is hearty enough to serve for lunch or dinner! Sometimes I add a cup of frozen green peas as soon as it is done cooking, which adds a bit more color and flavor! You don't have to wait for a rainy day or get a cold to enjoy Chicken Noodle Soup. This soup is good on any day! —Brenda*

1 medium onion, chopped

10 cups water

5 tablespoons McKay's Chicken Style Seasoning

1 tablespoon Better Than Bouillon No-Chicken Base

1 tablespoon parsley

1 cup carrots, sliced

1 cup celery, finely chopped

1 cup **Loma Linda**® Tender Bits, sliced in half lengthwise and diced

¼ cup quick barley

1 cup potatoes, peeled and diced

2 cups pasta noodles of your choice

Yield: 10 cups

(1 cup) Calories 140 Total Fat 1.5g Saturated Fat 0g Sodium 1020mg Total Carbohydrates 26g Fiber 3g Protein 6g

Hot Dog Soup

9 cups water

1 medium onion, chopped

5 cups cabbage, chopped

¼ cup McKay's Beef Style Seasoning

1 teaspoon salt

1 tablespoon Bragg Liquid Aminos

2 cups potatoes, diced

1 20-ounce can *Loma Linda*® Big Franks, sliced

Pour water in a stockpot and heat on medium high. Add onion, cabbage, McKay's Beef Style Seasoning, salt, and Bragg Liquid Aminos. Simmer until vegetables are tender, approximately 10 minutes, then add potatoes and cook for another 10 minutes. Add *Loma Linda*® Big Franks and serve hot.

*My grandsons, Michael and Jason, named this soup! They love **Loma Linda**® Big Franks, and one of their favorite things to do is roast them over a fire at my sister Cinda's house, whom they lovingly refer to as "Auntie Ceda." When I came up with this recipe, they eagerly contributed the name! Try adding a cup of sliced carrots or green peas, as it adds color without changing the flavor. —Brenda*

Yield: 14 1-cup servings

(1 cup) Calories 80 Total Fat 1.5g Saturated Fat 0g Sodium 780mg Total Carbohydrates 9g Fiber 3g Protein 8g

Vegetable Pasta Fagioli

In a large stockpot, sauté the onion, carrots, garlic, and **Loma Linda**® Tender Bits in the olive oil over medium heat until onion is clear. If the onion starts to stick, add a little water. Add the spices and tomatoes, and simmer until hot, then add the cannellini beans, pasta, spinach, and basil. Continue to simmer until hot and bubbly. Serve hot.

I really should have named this soup "Imagination Soup" because you can use your imagination when making it by adding different vegetables such as zucchini, yellow squash, chopped kale, butternut squash, potatoes, and just about any vegetable you happen to have on hand! Yes, that's right—just use your imagination! I think you get the idea . . . now let's get cooking! —Cinda

1 tablespoon extra virgin olive oil

1 medium onion, diced

1 cup carrots, diced

2 cloves fresh garlic, minced

1 19-ounce can *Loma Linda*® Tender Bits, cut into quarters

1 teaspoon salt (or to taste)

½ teaspoon red pepper flakes (or to taste)

3 28-ounce cans whole tomatoes

1 15-ounce can cannellini beans, drained

1½ cup cooked whole-wheat pasta (shells or corkscrew)

2 cups fresh spinach, chopped

2 tablespoons fresh basil, chopped

Yield: 14 1-cup servings

(1 cup) Calories 120 Total Fat 2.5g Saturated Fat 0g Sodium 650mg Total Carbohydrates 19g Fiber 5g Protein 8g

Black Bean Sausage Soup

1 cup water

4 cups canned tomatoes with the juice

1 cup onions, diced

½ teaspoon sea salt

¼ teaspoon cumin

1 teaspoon onion powder

1½ cups canned black beans

1 20-ounce can *Worthington*® Chili

1 cup Loma Linda Linketts, sliced

½ cup solid canned pumpkin

Place all the ingredients in a medium size kettle and cook for 20 to 25 minutes. Serve hot!

I made this recipe for one of our meat-eating friends, and he said he really liked it and asked me if the meat in the chili was pork. When I told him there was no meat in it at all he was shocked. I served it along with some homemade cornbread and sliced fresh tomatoes. I suggest making extra chili and invite the neighbors over to enjoy a special meal of fellowship! —Linda

Yield: 8 ½-cup servings

(½ cup) Calories 200 Total Fat 6g Saturated Fat 1g Sodium 850mg Total Carbohydrates 24g Fiber 8g Protein 13g

Roasted Ratatouille

Preheat oven to 425 degrees. Combine eggplant, fresh tomatoes, zucchini, onion, peppers, garlic, **Worthington® Vegetable Steaks™** strips, and oil in a large roasting pan. Sprinkle with salt to taste. Roast for 30 to 40 minutes or until vegetables are lightly browned and tender. Stir occasionally during roasting.

Stir in chickpeas, and roast for another 10 minutes. Remove from oven and stir in thyme, VegeSal, cayenne pepper, and canned tomatoes. Gently stir to combine thoroughly. Return to oven until heated and bubbly. Serve in bowls with your favorite type of rice or grain.

I love all the flavors and textures of this very thick and hearty stew. You can also serve it over pasta, quinoa, or polenta. Top with a dollop of soy sour cream and sprinkling of fresh thyme and oregano. This dish will keep several days in the refrigerator or several months in the freezer. —Cinda

1 medium eggplant, peeled and cut into 1–2 inch cubes

3 cups fresh Roma tomatoes, chopped

3 cups zucchini, cut into medium cubes

1 medium sweet onion, slivered

2 cups red yellow and orange baby peppers, cut into rings

3 cloves fresh garlic, minced

1 20-ounce can **Worthington® Vegetable Steaks™**, cut into small strips

3 tablespoons extra virgin olive oil

Salt to taste

1 16-ounce can chickpeas, drained and rinsed

2 teaspoons fresh or dried thyme

1 teaspoon VegeSal or an all-purpose vegetable seasoning

¼ teaspoon cayenne pepper

2 14.5-ounce cans petite diced tomatoes

Yield: 10 1-cup servings

(1 cup) Calories 170 Total Fat 6g Saturated Fat 0.5g Sodium 480mg Total Carbohydrates 20g Fiber 5g Protein 12g

Tijuana Minestrone

1 medium onion, diced

1 cup celery, diced

2 cups carrots, diced

2 tablespoons oil

3 cloves fresh garlic, minced

1 teaspoon dried or fresh thyme

½ teaspoon dried or fresh oregano

1 teaspoon salt (or to taste)

1 cup red bell pepper, diced

¼ cup Bragg Liquid Aminos

5 cups water

1 28-ounce can petite diced or crushed tomatoes

2 cups zucchini, diced

2 cups yellow squash, diced

1 16-ounce can dark red kidney beans, drained

1 16-ounce can garbanzo beans, drained

1 10-ounce package *Gardenburger* Black Bean Chipotle Veggie Burgers, cut into bite-sized pieces

2 cups fresh spinach, coarsely chopped

In a large stockpot over medium-high heat, sauté onion, celery, and carrots in oil until onion is clear. Add the garlic and spices and sauté another minute. Add the remaining ingredients, except spinach. Simmer on medium to low heat for approximately 20 minutes, or until vegetables are tender-firm. Add the spinach and stir to mix well. Remove from heat and serve hot.

You can substitute or add any other vegetable you like or happen to have on hand. You could also add some cooked pasta if you prefer, and some crushed red pepper for a little zing! —Cinda

Yield: 16 1-cup servings

(1 cup) Calories 110 Total Fat 3.5g Saturated Fat 0g Sodium 690mg Total Carbohydrates 19g Fiber 4g Protein 5g

Creamy Tender Bit Soup

Place all the ingredients, except for the Tofutti Better Than Sour Cream and parsley, in a large stockpot. When the vegetables are tender, remove from heat and blend in the Tofutti Better Than Sour Cream. Garnish with dried or fresh chopped parsley.

This quick and easy dish was a real hit with my family and friends. I love having delicious smells coming from my kitchen that make my family feel loved. It is also fun to share with friends and neighbors. Serve this delicious soup with a fresh salad, homemade bread, and a favorite dessert. —Linda

4 cups cabbage, finely chopped

1 cup carrots, shredded

2 cups onions, finely chopped

2 tablespoons McKay's Chicken Style Seasoning

½ teaspoon salt

1 19-ounce can *Loma Linda* Tender Bits, cut into medium-size pieces

1¼ cups potatoes, diced

½ cup Tofutti Better Than Sour Cream

½ teaspoon parsley, dried or fresh

Yield: 7 1-cup servings

(1 cup) Calories 180 Total Fat 5g Saturated Fat 0g Sodium 1050mg Total Carbohydrates 23g Fiber 5g Protein 10g

Chik'n Corn Chowder

6 cups water

1 cup onions, finely diced

1½ cups celery, finely diced

1 teaspoon celery salt

1 teaspoon onion powder

1 teaspoon sea salt

1 cup carrots, finely diced

2½ cups potatoes, finely diced

1½ cups cream style sweet corn

1 cup *Worthington® Vegetable Skallops®*, cut in small pieces

½ cup Tofutti Better Than Sour Cream

Place all the ingredients in a medium-sized pan on medium-high heat, except for the Tofutti Better Than Sour Cream. Cook until vegetables are tender. Stir in the Tofutti Better Than Sour Cream and serve!

This delicious corn chowder is a winner at our house! I like to serve it with homemade bread, fresh tomatoes, and green leafy lettuce from the garden. Soup is a welcoming meal for family and guests and is so easy to prepare! The savory smells of home will linger for a long time in their memories and make meal times around the dining room table a special place to be! —Linda

Yield: 9 1-cup servings

(1 cup) Calories 140 Total Fat 3g Saturated Fat 0g Sodium 830mg Total Carbohydrates 24g Fiber 3g Protein 6g

Potato Corn Chowder

In a skillet that has been sprayed with nonstick cooking spray, sauté *Loma Linda*® Tender Bits, onion, and celery over medium heat until onion is clear. In stockpot, place all the ingredients. Slowly simmer for 45 to 60 minutes. Serve hot!

There's nothing quite like a hot bowl of soup on a cold day. And this soup is so thick and hearty you can almost use a fork! I used agave nectar for a touch of sweetener, but you can also use sugar if you like. The Silk Soy Creamer makes it so smooth and creamy you'll almost think it's dairy. I like to store any leftover soup in a Mason jar. You can see instantly what it is and it takes up less space in the refrigerator! —Brenda

1 cup *Loma Linda*® Tender Bits, chopped

1 medium onion, chopped

½ cup celery, chopped

3 15-ounce cans cream style corn

1 cup unsweetened original almond milk

1 teaspoon fresh parsley

½ teaspoon celery salt

1½ cups potatoes, peeled and diced

2 teaspoons agave nectar

1 cup original Silk Soy Creamer

½ teaspoon salt

½ teaspoon red pepper flakes

Yield: 16 ½-cup servings

(½ cup) Calories 110 Total Fat 2g Saturated Fat 0g Sodium 400mg Total Carbohydrates 21g Fiber 2g Protein 4g

Seaside Chowder

1 small onion, diced

1 cup red bell pepper, diced

1 cup celery, diced

1 large bay leaf

1 tablespoon canola or extra virgin olive oil

2½ cups white potatoes, diced

1 20-ounce can *Worthington® Vegetable Skallops®*, drained and cut into bite-sized pieces

1 teaspoon dried tarragon

1 teaspoon dried or fresh thyme

½ teaspoon salt, or to taste

4 tablespoons McKay's Chicken Style Seasoning

4 cups vegetable stock

2½ cups fresh corn, cooked and cut off the cob

In a large stockpot, sauté the onion, red pepper, celery, bay leaf, and salt in the oil over medium-high heat until onion is clear. Add the remaining ingredients and cook on medium-low heat for approximately 15 to 20 minutes or until the potato is tender but still firm. Serve hot.

This is a great soup to make during corn season when you have lots of fresh corn on the cob. Of course you could use frozen corn, but I prefer the taste of the fresh! —Cinda

Yield: 12 1-cup servings

(1 cup) Calories 180 Total Fat 2.5g Saturated Fat 0g Sodium 1210mg Total Carbohydrates 22g Fiber 5g Protein 16g

Split Pea Soup

Place all ingredients in a stockpot. Slowly simmer for 45 to 60 minutes. Serve hot.

One of my favorite soups growing up was my mom's "Split Pea Soup." As with many of my recipes, she was definitely the inspiration for this one. It is a thicker soup, but if you prefer it thinner, just add a bit more water and extra McKay's Chicken Style Seasoning. I like to change it up a bit, so sometimes I add ½ cup quick barley or ½ cup diced potatoes, which are delicious too. This soup will thicken when cold, so when reheating leftovers, add just a little water to reach the right consistency. —Brenda

7 cups water

2 cups dried green peas

¼ cup McKay's Chicken Style Seasoning

½ teaspoon marjoram

½ teaspoon salt

¼ teaspoon cayenne pepper

1 medium onion, chopped

⅓ cup carrot, diced

1 19-ounce can *Loma Linda® Linketts™*, sliced

Yield: 16 ½-cup servings

(½ cup) Calories 140 Total Fat 3g Saturated Fat 0g Sodium 510mg Total Carbohydrates 18g Fiber 7g Protein 11g

Giambotta Stew

2 tablespoons extra virgin olive oil

3 cloves fresh garlic, minced

1 large sweet onion, diced

4 cups eggplant, diced

1 19-ounce can *Loma Linda* Little Links, cut into 1-inch pieces

2 28-ounce cans whole tomatoes

1 tablespoon dried oregano

2 teaspoons dried basil

1 teaspoon dried thyme

Salt to taste

½ teaspoon red pepper flakes

2 tablespoons McKay's Chicken Style Seasoning

1 cup celery, chopped

2 cups carrots, diced

2 cups potatoes, diced

2 cups zucchini, diced

2 cups yellow squash, diced

2 cups fresh spinach, chopped

¼ cup fresh or dried parsley

1 cup red bell pepper or Italian banana peppers, diced

1 15-ounce can cannellini beans, drained

In a large stockpot, sauté garlic, onions, eggplant, and the **Loma Linda** Little Links in the olive oil until the onion is clear. Add the remaining ingredients and simmer until vegetables are tender, approximately 20 to 25 minutes. Serve hot.

This is very similar to the Italian vegetable stew called Giambotta—hence the name! As you can see, it is a very hearty stew that is definitely a one-dish meal. I love to serve this in homemade bread bowls with a sprinkling of fresh chopped parsley. If you don't make bread, you can always purchase the personal-size round rolls and hollow them out. —Cinda

Yield: 20 1-cup servings

(1 cup) Calories 120 Total Fat 4g Saturated Fat 0.5g Sodium 410mg Total Carbohydrates 16g Fiber 5g Protein 7g

Lentil Link Stew

Sauté **Loma Linda**® Little Links over medium-high heat in a skillet that has been sprayed with nonstick cooking spray.

In stockpot, place water and salt. Add lentils, squeezed tomatoes with juice, and onions. Bring to a boil, then reduce to simmer and cook for 35 to 40 minutes. Add remaining ingredients and cook until vegetables are tender, approximately 10 to 15 minutes. Serve hot.

*Lentil soup was popular even in Bible times and is still loved today. It has such a wonderful flavor, and when you add the vegetables—you've got a complete meal! When squeezing whole tomatoes, I use latex gloves and break them up with my hands. Whole tomatoes yield more juice, so don't substitute diced canned tomatoes for whole tomatoes because the liquid measurements won't be the same. You can substitute other hot dogs, like **Loma Linda**® Big Franks or **Loma Linda**® Linketts™, if you prefer. —Brenda*

1 19-ounce can **Loma Linda**® Little Links, sliced

1 teaspoon salt

8 cups water

2 cups dried lentils

1 quart whole tomatoes, squeezed

1 medium onion, diced

1 teaspoon curry powder

½ teaspoon cumin

3 tablespoons McKay's Chicken Style Seasoning

⅛ teaspoon cayenne pepper (optional)

1 cup carrots, sliced

1 cup celery, diced

¼ cup quick barley

2 cups potatoes, peeled and coarsely chopped

½ teaspoon garlic powder

Yield: 16 1-cup servings

(1 cup) Calories 180 Total Fat 3.5g Saturated Fat 0.5g Sodium 610mg Total Carbohydrates 26g Fiber 10g Protein 12g

Skillet Beef Stew

1 20-ounce can *Worthington® Vegetable Steaks™*, sliced in half lengthwise and into bite-sized pieces

1 medium onion, chopped

1 cup celery, chopped

1 cup carrots, sliced thick

6 cups water

5 tablespoons McKay's Beef Style Seasoning

1 tablespoon Bragg Liquid Aminos

1 teaspoon Kitchen Bouquet

2 cups potatoes, coarsely chopped

Slurry:

2 tablespoons cornstarch

2 tablespoons cold water

Place **Worthington® Vegetable Steaks™** in a Ziploc bag containing flour. Shake to coat. Spray a skillet with nonstick cooking spray. Sauté steaks over medium-high heat until golden brown on both sides.

In a large saucepan, sauté onions in nonstick cooking spray over medium-high heat until clear. Add celery and carrots. Add water, McKay's Beef Style Seasoning, Bragg Liquid Aminos, and the Kitchen Bouquet. Simmer until carrots are almost tender, then add potatoes and simmer until potatoes are tender, about 10 minutes.

In a small container mix cornstarch and cold water to make the slurry. Pour into hot stew, stirring constantly. Add steaks and serve hot.

*Our mom is an awesome cook and she was determined to cook healthy meals for her kids. For that reason, we were raised vegetarian and practically grew up on **Loma Linda®** and **Worthington®** products. She made a dish we called "Steaks 'n' Tomatoes," which was basically **Worthington® Vegetable Steaks™** baked with slivered onions and Mom's home canned tomatoes on top. I still love it today and when I was experimenting with recipes for this cookbook, I tried turning this family recipe into a new one, and that's how Skillet Beef Stew was created. My new dilemma is . . . now I'm not sure which one is my favorite! —Brenda*

Yield: 10 1-cup servings

(1 cup) Calories 100 Total Fat 0.5g Saturated Fat 0g Sodium 960mg Total Carbohydrates 14g Fiber 2g Protein 9g

Pot Roast Stew

In a large kettle on medium-high heat, place all the ingredients except for the flour, ½ cup water, and canola oil. Simmer for approximately 25 to 30 minutes or until vegetables are tender.

Mix the flour, cold water, and canola oil together in a separate container until smooth and creamy. Stir the flour mixture into the stew and bring it to a boil. Remove from heat. Garnish with some fresh green onions.

I love one-dish meals because they make a simple meal seem so elegant! Just add a colorful fresh vegetable salad, and a special dessert to complete the meal. This stew is good served with homemade biscuits or it can be used to make a potpie. Just put the stew into a casserole dish and top with your favorite piecrust. Then invite some friends over and enjoy some good fellowship time. Many of our friendships were built over eating meals together in our home.
—*Linda*

8 cups water

1 cup onions, diced

1 cup celery, sliced diagonally

1 cup carrots, sliced diagonally

3 cups potatoes, coarsely chopped

2 teaspoons McKay's Beef Style Seasoning

6 tablespoons Bragg Liquid Aminos

1 20-ounce can *Worthington® Vegetable Skallops®*

½ cup unbleached all-purpose flour

½ cup cold water

2 tablespoons canola oil

Yield: 11 ½-cup servings

(½ cup) Calories 120 Total Fat 3g Saturated Fat 0g Sodium 770mg Total Carbohydrates 16g Fiber 3g Protein 9g

Steakhouse Stew

5 cups canned diced tomatoes

2 cups water

1 cup onions, diced

1 cup celery, diced

1 cup yellow pepper, diced

1 20-ounce can *Worthington® Vegetable Steaks™*, undrained

1 teaspoon sea salt

1 teaspoon McKay's Chicken Style Seasoning

½ teaspoon onion powder

2 cups potatoes, diced

In a medium-sized stockpot, place all the ingredients. Cook on medium-high heat for approximately 30 minutes or until vegetables are tender. Serve hot.

*Our family has always loved Mom's **Worthington® Vegetable Steaks™** baked in the oven with tomatoes and onions and served with potatoes. This delicious stew reminds me of some wonderful childhood memories of our family around our dining room table. Make up a pot of stew for your family and friends and enjoy a fun meal together.*
—Linda

Yield: 8 1-cup servings

(1 cup) Calories 120 Total Fat 1g Saturated Fat 0g Sodium 780mg Total Carbohydrates 18g Fiber 4g Protein 12g

Spicy Pepper Chili

In a large stockpot, add all ingredients except the pasta. Cook over medium-high heat until onions and peppers are tender. Add the cooked pasta and serve hot.

My husband loves the rich flavors in this chili and even enjoys eating it at breakfast time! He likes it both hot and cold! It can also be put in a Crock-Pot and then it is ready to eat when you come home. Either way it is delicious! Serve with cornbread and a fresh veggie tray.
—*Linda*

2 cups water

3 cups canned whole tomatoes, cut into medium pieces

½ cup onions, finely chopped

¼ cup green bell pepper, coarsely chopped

¼ cup sweet red pepper, coarsely chopped

¼ cup sweet yellow pepper, coarsely chopped

1 jalapeño pepper, sliced thin

1 20-ounce can *Worthington*® Chili

¼ teaspoon red pepper flakes

1 teaspoon sea salt

1 teaspoon onion powder

1 cup cooked tri-color rotini pasta

Yield: 8 1-cup servings

(1 cup) Calories 140 Total Fat 3.5g Saturated Fat 0.5g Sodium 790mg Total Carbohydrates 19g Fiber 4g Protein 9g

White Corn Chili

1 medium onion, diced

1 20-ounce can *Worthington*® Chili

4 cups canned tomatoes, with juice, squeezed

½ cup green chilies

1 15.5-ounce can great northern beans, drained

2 cups white corn

1 tablespoon chili powder

1 teaspoon sugar

1 teaspoon red pepper flakes

Sauté onion over medium-high heat in a skillet that has been sprayed with nonstick cooking spray. In stockpot, combine all ingredients and simmer for 15 minutes.

*When you don't have a lot of time, and you want to put together a good hot meal in a hurry, **Worthington**® Chili is the answer! It makes this dish come together in a snap! I love the white corn and northern beans that add a pop of color to this traditional tomato-based chili. You can even combine all the ingredients in a Crock-Pot and come home to a dinner that's ready to eat! —Brenda*

Yield: 16 ½-cup servings

(½ cup) Calories 130 Total Fat 2g Saturated Fat 0g Sodium 450mg Total Carbohydrates 24g Fiber 5g Protein 8g

Sweet Potato Chili

Place all the ingredients in a medium-sized kettle and cook until the sweet potatoes are tender. Serve with your favorite cornbread and fresh green salad.

I added sweet potatoes to this chili to give it more nutrition. It has been found that just one cup serving of sweet potatoes contains 65 percent of the minimum necessary daily amount of vitamin C. Sweet potatoes are also high in calcium, foliate, potassium, and beta-carotene. Sweet potatoes have been listed as the number one most nutritious vegetable because they are so nutritionally rich. So cook up a batch of chili and enjoy not only some good-tasting food but great nutrition as well. —Linda

4 cups water

1 cup onion, finely diced

½ teaspoon salt

¼ teaspoon cayenne pepper

2 20-ounce cans *Worthington*® Chili

½ cup mild thick and chunky salsa

½ teaspoon seasoned salt

3 cups sweet potatoes, cut in
     medium-sized pieces

Yield: 10 1-cup servings

(1 cup) Calories 210 Total Fat 5g Saturated Fat 1g Sodium 790mg Total Carbohydrates 27g Fiber 6g Protein 13g

Chili Mac

1 large onion, diced

2 cloves fresh garlic, minced

½ cup water

2 20-ounce cans *Worthington*® Chili

4 cups cooked corkscrew whole-wheat pasta

1 7-ounce can diced green chilies

1 tablespoon ground cumin

1 tablespoon chili powder

1 14.5-ounce can stewed or chili style tomatoes

½ cup Reduced Fat Vegenaise

Salt to taste

In a large saucepan, sauté the onion and garlic in water until onion is clear. Add the spices and salt and stir to mix well. Add the remaining ingredients and gently stir to combine. Continue to cook until thoroughly heated. Serve hot with crumbled tortilla chips over the top.

This is one of those fast and easy dishes that everyone will love. If you are like my family, you can add some cayenne pepper or hot sauce to give it some zip! I like to serve it with cornbread and a salad, but if you want to get fancy you can serve it in cornbread bowls! —Cinda

Yield: 28 ½-cup servings

(½ cup) Calories 170 Total Fat 5g Saturated Fat 0.5g Sodium 390mg Total Carbohydrates 22g Fiber 3g Protein 8g

Entrées and Side Dishes

Farro Fried Rice
p. 110

Roasted
Acorn Squash
p. 108

Spicy Hickory Riblets
p. 112

Campfire
Baked Beans
p. 127

Fried Skallops
p. 113

New Orleans Gumbo
p. 126

Roasted Acorn Squash

3 medium acorn squash, cut in half
  and seeded

Rice Filling:

2 medium sweet onions, diced

1 cup celery, finely chopped

1 19-ounce can *Loma Linda*® Tender
  Bits, cut into small pieces

2 teaspoons dried sage

1 tablespoon extra virgin olive oil

Salt to taste

2 cups wild rice blend, cooked
  according to directions

1½ cups pecans, roughly chopped and
  toasted

1 cup dried cranberries

Cranberry Pomegranate Juice:

1 cup pomegranate juice

¾ cup pure maple syrup

1 teaspoon ground cinnamon

3 cups fresh or frozen cranberries

Preheat oven to 400 degrees. Spray acorn squash halves with a nonstick cooking spray and place cut side down on a parchment or foil lined baking sheet. Bake for 40 to 45 minutes, or until tender. Remove from oven and fill with the rice mixture. Return to oven for 10 minutes. Remove and place on individual serving plates. Drizzle with the cranberry pomegranate sauce and serve.

For Rice Filling: In a large skillet sauté the onions, celery, **Loma Linda**® Tender Bits, and sage in oil over medium heat until onion is clear. Add salt to taste and mix in the cooked rice blend, pecans, and dried cranberries. Stir to mix. Remove from heat.

For Cranberry Pomegranate Juice: Place all ingredients in a medium saucepan, cover, and bring to a boil, watching carefully to make sure it does not boil over. Uncover and cook at a rapid simmer for 15 to 20 minutes, stirring often, until the cranberries have burst and the liquid has reduced enough to become saucy. Serve at room temperature.

You can also use this filling in other varieties of squash. My husband loves it with the butternut squash. He also likes some hot sauce added to the cranberry pomegranate sauce. —Cinda

Yield: 12 ¼-stuffed squash

(¼ squash) Calories 370 Total Fat 12g Saturated Fat 1.5g Sodium 330mg Total Carbohydrates 61g Fiber 9g Protein 11g

Vegetable Delight Fried Rice

In a large skillet that has been sprayed with nonstick cooking spray, sauté onion, celery, and **Worthington® Vegetable Skallops®** over medium heat until onion is clear and the **Worthington® Vegetable Skallops®** are lightly browned. Add the seasoning and the remaining ingredients, except the sesame oil. Mix well and continue sautéing for approximately 4 minutes, stirring frequently to avoid burning and sticking. Drizzle with the sesame oil and stir until well mixed. Serve hot.

I love fried rice, but I don't like all the fat and calories it normally has. This recipe is delicious without all the oil, fat, and calories! You can add whatever vegetables you like and can also substitute tofu or your favorite vegan meat substitute. It tastes good served hot, room temperature, or I like to even eat this cold! Try it today, I bet you won't miss all that oil either! —Cinda

1 cup celery, diced

1 medium onion, diced

1 20-ounce can **Worthington® Vegetable Skallops®**, cut into thin strips

3 tablespoons oriental vegetable seasoning, or to taste

2 cups fresh broccoli florets

1½ cups carrots, cut into thin slivers

1 cup snow peas, cut into thirds

4 cups cooked brown rice

2 teaspoons dark sesame oil

Yield: 18 ½-cup servings

(½ cup) Calories 80 Total Fat 1g Saturated Fat 0g Sodium 230mg Total Carbohydrates 13g Fiber 2g Protein 5g

Farro Fried Rice

1 medium onion, slivered finely

1 clove garlic, minced

½ teaspoon red pepper flakes

2 cups *Worthington® Vegetable Skallops®*, chopped

1 cup sweet red pepper, diced

1 cup fresh mushrooms, sliced

1 cup pea pods, sliced diagonally

1 cup small broccoli florets

2 cups cooked farro

2 tablespoons Bragg Liquid Aminos

2 teaspoons McKay's Chicken Style Seasoning

1 tablespoon pure sesame oil

Spray a stockpot with nonstick cooking spray. Add onion, garlic, red pepper flakes, and *Worthington® Vegetable Skallops®*. Sauté over medium heat until onion is clear, then add sweet red pepper, mushrooms, pea pods, and broccoli florets. Stir in the cooked farro, Bragg Liquid Aminos, and McKay's Chicken seasoning. Cook until the vegetable are tender, approximately 10 minutes. Drizzle the sesame oil over the top and toss.

Farro is the oldest cultivated grain in the world, dating all the way back to Bible times. It is a whole grain that is an excellent source for complex carbohydrates and has twice the fiber and protein of modern wheat. Just to name a few of its health benefits, farro has been found to stimulate the immune system, lower cholesterol, and help maintain blood sugar levels. I not only love this grain because it tastes so good, but it is one of the most nutritious grains you can eat. It can be used interchangeably with brown rice, although farro has a chewier texture. Given the choice between brown rice and farro, I'd choose farro every time! I love it! —Brenda

Yield: 8 ½-cup servings

(½ cup) Calories 140 Total Fat 2.5g Saturated Fat 0g Sodium 560mg Total Carbohydrates 20g Fiber 5g Protein 12g

BBQ Ribs Over Farro

Puree diced tomatoes in a food processor until smooth. Set aside. Spray a medium saucepan with a nonstick cooking spray. Add onion and sauté over medium-high heat until clear. Add pureed tomatoes, ketchup, brown sugar, Worcestershire sauce, Bragg Liquid Aminos, lemon juice, and tomato paste. Mix well, then simmer uncovered on low for 30 minutes. Break **MorningStar Farms®** Hickory BBQ Riblets apart and add to sauce. Serve over farro.

*I love the barbecue flavor of these **MorningStar Farms**® Hickory BBQ Riblets so much that honestly, they would be good right out of the package. But to shake things up a bit, I created this recipe and made it a little saucier to go over the farro. I love the tangy goodness of the sauce and, combined with the farro, it's a perfect combination!*
—Brenda

1 14.5-ounce can petite diced tomatoes

¼ cup onion, finely diced

1 cup ketchup

3 tablespoons brown sugar

2 tablespoons vegetarian Worcestershire sauce

2 teaspoons Bragg Liquid Aminos

2 tablespoons fresh lemon juice

4 teaspoons double concentrated tomato paste

3 10-ounce packages *MorningStar Farms*® Hickory BBQ Riblets, without sauce

6 cups cooked farro

Yield: 6 cups BBQ ribs; 6 cups farro

(½ cup ribs & ½ cup farro) Calories 190 Total Fat 0.5g Saturated Fat 0g Sodium 300mg Total Carbohydrates 44g Fiber 5g Protein 8g

Spicy Hickory Riblets

1 cup canned diced tomatoes

1½ cups hot water

1 cup onions, chopped

1 cup sweet banana peppers

½ cup hot banana peppers

1 cup carrots, slivered

Salt to taste

½ teaspoon McKay's Chicken Style Seasoning

1 cup zucchini, sliced and halved

2 cups *MorningStar Farms*® Hickory BBQ Riblets, including sauce

2 cups cooked brown rice

Place all the ingredients in a large skillet except the zucchini, *MorningStar Farms*® Hickory BBQ Riblets, and rice. Cook on medium-high heat until the vegetables are crunchy tender. Add the zucchini and cook until crunchy tender, approximately 5 minutes. Break the riblets into large pieces and gently stir in to the vegetables. Serve hot over steamed brown rice.

I made this dish for my dad, and he took a bite and said I don't give out compliments too easy but this one is a winner! Serve these delicious riblets over brown rice or your favorite noodles. I like to serve it with a fresh vegetable salad and homemade bread. —Linda

Yield: 5 1-cup servings

(1 cup) Calories 220 Total Fat 2.5g Saturated Fat 0g Sodium 710mg Total Carbohydrates 42g Fiber 7g Protein 11g

Fried Skallops

Mix the almond milk with the cornstarch and set aside. Slice the thicker **Worthington® Vegetable Skallops®** in half and dip in the almond milk mixture then in the cracker crumbs. Place the canola oil in a large skillet and heat over medium hot. Sauté **Worthington® Vegetable Skallops®** until golden brown on each side. Serve with the Honey Mustard Sauce.

For Honey Mustard Sauce: Mix all ingredients together in a small bowl.

This is one of my childhood favorites that Mom would make for a special treat when we were growing up. There were never any leftovers at our house! I like to serve it with homemade mashed potatoes and gravy, vegetables, salad, and a homemade dessert. Enjoy! —Linda

½ cup unsweetened original almond milk

3 tablespoons cornstarch

1 20-ounce can *Worthington® Vegetable Skallops®*

1 cup cracker crumbs

¼ cup canola oil

Honey Mustard Sauce:

¼ cup Grapeseed Vegenaise

¼ cup Tofutti Better Than Sour Cream

2 teaspoons prepared yellow mustard

1 tablespoon agave nectar

Yield: 42 Skallops; 10 tablespoons sauce

(3 skallops) Calories 90 Total Fat 5g Saturated Fat 0g Sodium 170mg Total Carbohydrates 5g Fiber >1g Protein 5g

(1 tablespoon sauce) Calories 60 Total Fat 4.5g Saturated Fat 0g Sodium 75mg Total Carbohydrates 3g Fiber 0g Protein 0g

Baked Chicken Patties

Gravy:

4 cups water

4 teaspoons McKay's Chicken Style Seasoning

½ teaspoon sea salt

½ teaspoon onion powder

1 tablespoon soy margarine

½ cup cornstarch

½ cup cold water

½ cup Tofutti Better Than Sour Cream

Chicken Patties:

1 cup water

½ teaspoon salt

2 cups onions, slivered

1 cup red peppers, slivered

2 9.5-ounce packages *MorningStar Farms® Grillers®* Chik'n Veggie Patties

½ cup seasoned bread crumbs

In a medium-sized kettle on high heat bring the water, McKay's Chicken Style Seasoning, sea salt, onion powder, and soy margarine to a boil. In a small container, mix the cornstarch with the cold water together until it is well blended. Slowly pour the slurry into the kettle, stirring rapidly. When thickened, remove from heat and stir in the Better Than Sour Cream. Set aside.

Add the water and salt to a medium-sized skillet. Add onions and red peppers and sauté over medium heat until all the water is gone. Spray a separate large skillet with nonstick cooking spray and heat over medium high. Bread the *MorningStar Farms® Grillers®* Chik'n Veggie Patties with the seasoned bread crumbs, place in the hot skillet, and cook on both sides.

Spray a 9 x 13-inch baking dish with nonstick cooking spray and spread approximately 2 cups of the gravy on the bottom. Lay the patties on the gravy, then cover with the remaining gravy. Top with onions and red peppers, then bake at 350 degrees for approximately 20 to 25 minutes. Serve hot.

*One of the students at Great Lakes Adventist Academy, Steven Wagner, came over to see me. I asked him if he would like to try these delicious **MorningStar Farms® Grillers®** Chik'n Veggie Patties and he said sure! He liked this dish so much that I sent the whole pan back with him to the dorm. Serve with baked potatoes, fresh broccoli, homemade dinner rolls, sliced tomatoes, a raw vegetable tray, and homemade pie. —Linda*

Yield: 8 patties; 10 ½-cup servings gravy

(1 patty and gravy) Calories 210 Total Fat 7g Saturated Fat 0.5g Sodium 1140mg Total Carbohydrates 27g Fiber 5g Protein 11g

Old-Fashioned Meatloaf

In a large skillet, add the water, onion, and McKay's Chicken Style Seasoning. Sauté on medium heat until the onion is clear. Remove from heat and set aside. Combine the flaxseed meal and the ⅓ cup of water and set aside for 5 minutes.

In a large mixing bowl, place the **Loma Linda® Vege-Burger®**, Bragg Liquid Aminos, and VegeSal seasoning. Stir to combine well. Add the tofu, bread crumbs, oats, nuts, and Vegenaise. Mix well, then add the flaxseed mixture and the sautéed onions. Gently stir to completely combine.

Spray a 9 x 13-inch casserole with a nonstick cooking spray and pour the mixture into the center of the dish. Form into a rectangle leaving ½-inch space on all sides. Combine the ketchup, Sriracha sauce, and brown sugar in a small bowl and pour over the top. Spread evenly to cover. Mix the tomato soup with the water (or per directions on the can) and pour around the sides of the meatloaf. Bake in a 375-degree oven for 45 minutes or until firm and top is a little crusty. Slice and serve hot.

This is one of my favorite meatloaves! Since it freezes well, I almost always have one in my freezer ready to pull out and bake when unexpected company arrives. My family loves to eat the leftovers the next day in a sandwich, that is if there is any left over! —Cinda

½ cup water

1 large onion, diced

1 tablespoon McKay's Chicken Style Seasoning

2 tablespoons flaxseed meal

⅓ cup water

1 19-ounce can *Loma Linda® Vege-Burger®*

2 tablespoons Bragg Liquid Aminos

2 teaspoons VegeSal

1 14-ounce package water-packed firm tofu, drained

1 cup bread crumbs

2 cups quick oats

2 cups walnuts, finely diced

2 cups pecans, finely diced

3 tablespoons Reduced Fat Vegenaise

1 cup ketchup

2 teaspoons Sriracha hot chili sauce

1 tablespoon brown sugar

1 10¾-ounce can tomato soup

1 cup water

Yield: 24 slices

(1 slice) Calories 270 Total Fat 16g Saturated Fat 1.5g Sodium 550mg Total Carbohydrates 21g Fiber 4g Protein 12g

Vegetable Pad Thai

4 cups rice noodles

2 cups onions, finely diced

1 cup fresh mushrooms, sliced

1 tablespoon red curry paste

½ teaspoon salt

½ teaspoon cayenne pepper

1½ cups *Worthington® Vegetable Skallops®*

¼ cup sweet red pepper, slivered

¼ cup sweet yellow pepper, slivered

¼ cup sweet orange pepper, slivered

1 cup broccoli florets

2 teaspoons sesame oil

½ cup whole peanuts

Lime slices

Peanut Butter Sauce:

3 tablespoons crunchy natural peanut butter

1 tablespoon agave nectar

1 teaspoon fresh lime juice

3 tablespoons Bragg Liquid Aminos

1 teaspoon fresh ginger, grated

Cook the rice noodles according to package directions. Rinse and set aside. In a large skillet on medium-high heat, sauté the onions, mushrooms, and seasonings in a little water for approximately 15 minutes. Add the **Worthington® Vegetable Skallops®**, peppers, and broccoli and cook until tender crunchy. Stir in the rice noodles and peanut butter sauce. Drizzle with the sesame oil. Garnish the top with whole peanuts and lime slices.

For Peanut Butter Sauce: Combine all ingredients in a small saucepan. Heat over medium heat until hot and bubbly.

Pad Thai is not only easy to make but delicious too. For a more intense flavor, sauté with 2 cloves of grated or minced garlic. It makes a great entrée not only for the family but for guests as well. —Linda

Yield: 16 ½-cup servings

(½ cup) Calories 180 Total Fat 2.5g Saturated Fat 0g Sodium 360mg Total Carbohydrates 36g Fiber <1g Protein 5g

Chicken Pad Thai

Soak noodles in boiling hot water for 25 to 30 minutes until noodles are al dente. Spray a large skillet with nonstick cooking spray and sauté onion and **Loma Linda®** Tender Bits over medium heat until onion is clear. Add peanut sauce and noodles to skillet and mix thoroughly. Top with chopped peanuts.

For Peanut Sauce: Add all ingredients to blender and process until smooth.

*I really love Thai food and Pad Thai is an all time favorite. Most Pad Thai I've eaten is plain but I love the added texture that the **Loma Linda®** Tender Bits give. Don't skip the step of sautéing with the onions as that really flavors the Tender Bits. I usually make a double batch of the peanut sauce because I like to drizzle extra over the top. It's also a great dipping sauce for the fresh spring rolls I usually serve with it! —Brenda*

3 cups cooked Thai rice noodles

1 medium onion, diced

1 20-ounce can *Loma Linda®* Tender Bits, sliced in thin strips

Peanut Sauce:

½ cup Silk coconut milk

¼ cup agave nectar

1 teaspoon Bragg Liquid Aminos

⅓ cup fresh lemon juice

½ teaspoon red pepper flakes

½ cup peanut butter

½ teaspoon garlic powder

1 tablespoon Thai chili paste

½ teaspoon coriander

½ teaspoon cumin

⅛ teaspoon salt

Yield: 12 ½-cup servings

(½ cup) Calories 180 Total Fat 6g Saturated Fat 1g Sodium 360mg Total Carbohydrates 24g Fiber 2g Protein 8g

Vegetable Green Curry

3 13.5-ounce cans lite or regular coconut milk

2 tablespoons green curry paste

2 tablespoons dark brown sugar

2 tablespoons Bragg Liquid Aminos

1 cup carrots, thinly sliced

2 cups small new potatoes, thinly sliced

3 cups fresh asparagus, cut into 2-inch pieces

2 cups fresh snow peas

½ cup fresh Thai or regular basil leaves, cut into slivers

1 20-ounce can *Worthington® Vegetable Skallops®*, cut into medium-sized cubes

In a large kettle over medium-high heat, whisk together coconut milk, green curry paste, brown sugar, and the Bragg Liquid Aminos. Bring to a gentle boil and add the carrots and potatoes. Cook until vegetables are almost tender and then add the remaining ingredients. Cook for approximately 3 minutes longer. Serve hot over brown rice.

This is one of my new favorite curries! I love the combination of vegetables. Green curry is known to be one of the more spicy curries, so if you like a more mild curry you can use a red or yellow Thai curry paste instead of the green. —Cinda

Yield: 24 ½-cup servings

(½ cup) Calories 110 Total Fat 7g Saturated Fat 6g Sodium 210mg Total Carbohydrates 9g Fiber <1g Protein 5g

Curried Lentil Pies

In a skillet sprayed with nonstick cooking spray, sauté **Loma Linda**® Little Links over medium heat and set aside.

Place all ingredients, except potatoes, carrots, and pastry in a stockpot. Cook on medium heat for approximately one hour or until tender. Add potatoes and carrots 15 minutes before lentils are completely done, and cook till tender.

Sprinkle counter with flour. Prepare crust by rolling out a puffed pastry sheet. Cut out two circles approximately ½-inch bigger than a 4-inch mini pie tin. Place one inside the pie tin. Add 1 cup of filling. Cover with second puff pastry circle and crimp the edges together. Bake at 400 degrees for 30 minutes.

*I travel to Australia quite often for speaking appointments and my friends, Kevin and Jenny Maevsky, took me to their favorite "pie" place. Being from America, I was thinking dessert! They found it quite amusing to see the look on my face when I saw all the savory pies on display! There were mini-pies of all kinds, including a wide assortment of meat pies, which of course I didn't try. I did however fall in love with their lentil pies, which were amazing! I came straight home and created this dish adding **Loma Linda**® Little Links for added texture, protein, and flavor! Now I don't even miss those pies, although I miss my friends Kevin and Jenny very much!*
—*Brenda*

2 cups petite diced tomatoes

4 cups water

1½ teaspoons salt

1 cup lentils, uncooked

1 cup *Loma Linda*® Little Links, sliced

1 medium onion, diced fine

2½ teaspoons red curry powder

½ teaspoon garlic powder

4 teaspoons double-concentrated tomato paste

1 cup potatoes, diced

½ cup carrots, sliced

1 17.3-ounce package puff pastry sheets, thawed

Yield: 6 mini pies

(¼ pie) Calories 190 Total Fat 10g Saturated Fat 2.5g Sodium 320mg Total Carbohydrates 18g Fiber 4g Protein 7g

Tamale Vegetable Casserole

2 cups instant corn masa mix

1½ teaspoons Rumford baking powder

1 teaspoon salt

1 teaspoon McKay's Chicken Style Seasoning

1 tablespoon nutritional yeast flakes

1 cup water

⅔ cup canola oil

1 medium onion, diced

2 cloves fresh garlic, minced

1 tablespoon canola oil

1 19-ounce can *Loma Linda® Vege-Burger®*

1 teaspoon ground cumin

1 teaspoon oregano

½ teaspoon garlic powder

½ teaspoon onion powder

½ teaspoon red pepper flakes

½ cup red bell pepper, diced

1 cup yellow squash, diced

2 cups zucchini, diced

1 cup frozen or fresh sweet corn

1 cup tomato, peeled and chopped

1 15-ounce can black beans, drained and rinsed

Mix the first 5 ingredients in a medium mixing bowl and stir to combine. Pour in the water and oil and stir until well blended. Set aside.

In a large skillet, sauté the onion and garlic over medium-high heat in the canola oil until onion is clear. Add the **Loma Linda® Vege-Burger®** and spices and continue to sauté until browned. Set aside.

Spray another large skillet generously with a nonstick cooking spray. Sauté the red bell pepper, zucchini, yellow squash, corn, and tomato over medium heat until vegetables are firm but tender. Stir in the black beans and set aside.

Spray a 7 x 11-inch 2-quart baking dish with a nonstick cooking spray. Place half of the corn masa mixture in the bottom and pat evenly to cover the bottom of the casserole dish. Top with the **Loma Linda® Vege-Burger®** mixture and pat down firmly. Next add all of the vegetable mixture and press down firmly. Top with the remaining corn masa mixture and gently press down firmly and evenly to completely cover the vegetables. Cover the casserole with foil, making sure to press the edges to seal. Fill a larger baking dish with approximately 2 inches of water and place the casserole dish in the middle. Bake in a preheated 375-degree oven for 50 minutes. Remove from oven and cut into 8 pieces and serve hot.

My husband loved this casserole. Of course, he put hot sauce and a spicy salsa on his! You can serve this with all of your favorite traditional Mexican toppings like salsa, vegan sour cream, and avocado. I actually liked it just as it is, without any toppings, because I love the taste of the corn masa. —Cinda

Yield: 8 squares

(1 square) Calories 310 Total Fat 6g Saturated Fat 0.5g Sodium 810mg Total Carbohydrates 43g Fiber 9g Protein 20g

Chicken Vegetable Alfredo

In a large skillet on medium-high heat, put the water, sea salt, onions, garlic, mushrooms, sea salt, and carrots. Cook until crunchy tender. When almost done add the **Worthington® Vegetable Skallops®**, zucchini, and yellow squash. Steam until the vegetables are almost done, then remove from heat.

Pour the milk into a medium-sized kettle and heat over medium-high heat. Add the ½ teaspoon of salt and the seasoned salt. In a small bowl, mix the cold water and cornstarch. Stir until well mixed. When the milk is hot, slowly stir the cornstarch slurry into the hot milk. Continuing stirring until it thickens. Remove from heat and add the Better Than Sour Cream and Parmesan cheese. Pour over the vegetables and gently stir until well mixed. Serve over your favorite pasta.

When we were growing up, Mom made something like this using dairy products. I am constantly finding even healthier ways to serve some of our old favorites to my own family. Serve this Chicken Vegetable Alfredo over brown rice or your favorite pasta. Add a cup of steamed broccoli to the alfredo to add more color and nutrition. Serve it with a fresh vegetable salad and strawberry shortcake.
—Linda

1½ cup water

1 teaspoon sea salt

1 cup onions, finely diced

1 clove fresh garlic, minced

1 cup fresh mushrooms, sliced (optional)

1 cup carrots, sliced

2 cups **Worthington® Vegetable Skallops®**, cut into strips

1 cup yellow squash, sliced

1 cup zucchini, sliced

4 cups original soymilk or almond milk

½ teaspoon sea salt

1 teaspoon seasoned salt

½ cup cornstarch

½ cup water

1 cup Tofutti Better Than Sour Cream

¼ cup grated vegan Parmesan cheese

Yield: *10 ½-cup servings*

(½ cup) Calories 190 Total Fat 7g Saturated Fat 1g Sodium 820mg Total Carbohydrates 21g Fiber 2g Protein 12g

Turkey Tetrazzini

½ pound spaghetti

1 medium onion, diced

1 20-ounce can *Worthington®
Vegetable Skallops®*, sliced thin
lengthwise

4 cups fresh mushrooms, sliced

2 cloves fresh garlic, minced

1 teaspoon fresh parsley, minced

4 cups unsweetened original almond
milk

1½ tablespoons Better Than Bouillon
No-Chicken Base

½ teaspoon Italian seasoning

2 tablespoons fresh lemon juice

Slurry:

2 tablespoons cornstarch

2 tablespoons cold water

Cook spaghetti according to package directions. Spray a skillet with nonstick cooking spray and sauté onion and *Worthington® Vegetable Skallops®* over medium-high heat until onion is clear. Add mushrooms and sauté until tender. Then add garlic and sauté until mushroom juices are reduced. Add parsley, almond milk, Better Than Bouillon No-Chicken Base, Italian seasoning, and fresh lemon juice. Simmer for 5 minutes, then slowly add prepared slurry, stirring constantly. Cook until thickened, then add cooked spaghetti.

For Slurry: In a small container, stir together cornstarch and water.

*I love just about any kind of pasta but especially spaghetti or angel hair. This tetrazzini has a creamy white sauce similar to alfredo, yet with a twist of its own. And as an added bonus, no heavy cream! The **Worthington® Vegetable Skallops®** have a nice texture, and the Better Than Bouillon No-Chicken Base gives a wonderful flavor. You can use your favorite vegan chicken bouillon, but, in my book, this one is the best! —Brenda*

Yield: 8 1-cup servings

(1 cup) Calories 190 Total Fat 2.5g Saturated Fat 0g Sodium 650mg Total Carbohydrates 30g Fiber 3g Protein 15g

Tender Bit Primavera

Place all the ingredients in a skillet, except for the pasta. Simmer on medium heat until the onions and peppers are tender. Serve hot over angel hair pasta.

This dish can also be made in a Crock-Pot so that it is all ready when everyone comes home at the end of a long day; all you have to do is add the pasta. The pasta can be cooked the night before. Just rinse it in cold water and put it in an airtight container or a Ziploc bag. The primavera is also good with eggplant cooked in the sauce. I like to cut it in cubes and leave the skin on for extra nutrition. This dish is even better the second time around—if there are any leftovers to serve!
—Linda

1 cup onions, diced

1 cup sweet yellow pepper, chopped

1 cup water

2 cup whole tomatoes, crushed

2 cups tomato sauce

2 cups spaghetti sauce

½ teaspoon red pepper flakes

1 19-ounce can *Loma Linda*® Tender Bits, chopped

1 teaspoon onion powder

¼ teaspoon garlic powder

6 cups cooked angel hair pasta

Salt to taste

Yield: 12 1-cup servings

(1 cup) Calories 200 Total Fat 3g Saturated Fat 0g Sodium 920mg Total Carbohydrates 33g Fiber 5g Protein 10g

Mexican Spaghetti

1 13.25-ounce package whole-wheat
thin spaghetti

1 tablespoon extra virgin olive oil

1 medium onion, chopped

6 *Gardenburger*® Black Bean Chipotle
Veggie Burgers

1 14.5-ounce can petite-diced
tomatoes

2 4.5-ounce cans diced green chilies

1 cup mild or medium salsa

1 teaspoon ground cumin

Salt to taste

1 15-ounce can black beans, drained
and rinsed

Cook spaghetti according to package directions and set aside. Heat oil in a large skillet and sauté onions over medium heat until clear. Add a little water if needed to prevent browning. Crumble the burgers and add to the onions, along with the tomatoes, green chilies, salsa, cumin, salt, and black beans. Stir to combine and continue sautéing another 5 minutes. Add the cooked spaghetti and mix well. Serve right away or place in a baking dish and refrigerate. When ready to serve, bake at 375 degrees for 20 to 30 minutes or until thoroughly heated.

This is a great dish to make for those church potlucks! It is easy to make and has lots of flavor as well as nutrition. I serve it with crushed tortilla chips on top and garnish with fresh-diced tomatoes and avocado. You can also add sliced black olives. —Cinda

Yield: 14 1-cup servings

(1 cup) Calories 190 Total Fat 3g Saturated Fat 0g Sodium 490mg Total Carbohydrates 36g Fiber 5g Protein 7g

Vegetable Ziti

Spray a stockpot with nonstick cooking spray. Add onion and garlic and sauté over medium-high heat until onion is clear. Add yellow sweet pepper, mushrooms, and asparagus and sauté until tender. Add tomatoes, red pepper flakes, water, McKay's Chicken Seasoning, and *MorningStar Farms® Grillers®* Chik'n Veggie Patties. Simmer for 15 minutes. Add cooked ziti.

*Vegetables are so good for us and this recipe has a nice variety and an attractive assortment of color as well. You can try other vegetables too, such as green peas, green beans, or even cubed eggplant. This is your basic ziti dish, but the star ingredient is the **MorningStar Farms® Grillers®** Chik'n Veggie Patties. It has a nice balance of texture and flavor without overpowering the recipe. Serve with some fresh Italian bread and imagine you are in a quaint little restaurant in Italy!*
—Brenda

1 medium onion, diced

1 clove garlic, minced

½ cup sweet yellow pepper, diced

1 cup fresh mushrooms, sliced

1½ cups fresh asparagus, cut into 2½-inch pieces

1 cup petite diced tomatoes

½ teaspoon red pepper flakes

1 cup water

1 tablespoon McKay's Chicken Style Seasoning

1 9.5-ounce package *MorningStar Farms® Grillers®* Chik'n Veggie Patties, cut into strips

1 cup cooked ziti

Yield: 6 1-cup servings

(1 cup) Calories 140 Total Fat 2g Saturated Fat 0g Sodium 650mg Total Carbohydrates 17g Fiber 3g Protein 15g

New Orleans Gumbo

1 medium onion, slivered finely

1 clove garlic, minced

½ teaspoon red pepper flakes

1 cup *Worthington® Vegetable Skallops®*, sliced in half lengthwise and crosswise

2 cups canned tomatoes

3 cups fresh okra, sliced

½ cup sweet yellow pepper, coarsely chopped

1 tablespoon McKay's Chicken Style Seasoning

1 teaspoon agave nectar

Spray a stockpot with nonstick cooking spray. Add onion, garlic, red pepper flakes, and *Worthington® Vegetable Skallops®*. Sauté over medium heat until onion is clear, then add the remaining ingredients. Simmer for 15 minutes. Serve over grits or brown rice.

Years ago, I spent a week in New Orleans for a nursing convention and was introduced to Cajun cooking. Everywhere I ate, there seemed to be some sort of gumbo on every menu. Surprisingly enough, there were some restaurants that offered a vegetarian gumbo, which I thoroughly enjoyed. I came home and started experimenting with different gumbo dishes and came up with this one that my whole family loved. The **Worthington® Vegetable Skallops®** *add just enough chewiness that even shrimp eaters would love!* —Brenda

Yield: 5 1-cup servings

(1 cup) Calories 110 Total Fat 0.5g Saturated Fat 0g Sodium 630mg Total Carbohydrates 16g Fiber 5g Protein 9g

Campfire Baked Beans

In a large bowl, mix all ingredients together, then pour into a large deep baking dish. Bake at 375 degrees for 45 to 60 minutes or until bubbly and thickened.

This is my family's favorite baked beans. It is great to take on picnics because is good hot, room temperature, OR even cold! Believe it or not . . . I love it in a sandwich with just butter or the Grapeseed Vegenaise! And yes, you can make it over a fire when you are camping! —Cinda

1 28-ounce can vegetarian baked beans

1 16-ounce can dark red kidney beans, drained but not rinsed

1 15.8-ounce can great northern beans, drained but not rinsed

1 16-ounce can pinto beans, drained but not rinsed

1 20-ounce can *Loma Linda®️ Linketts™*, cut into ½-inch pieces

½ cup dark brown sugar

1½ cups ketchup

1 tablespoon prepared mustard

2 tablespoons vegetarian Worcestershire sauce

Yield: 15 1-cup servings

(1 cup) Calories 230 Total Fat 3.5g Saturated Fat 0.5g Sodium 400mg Total Carbohydrates 40g Fiber 6g Protein 13g

Sausage Vegetable Pizza

½ cup water

1½ cups onions, thinly sliced

3 cups spaghetti sauce

1 cup yellow squash, sliced into
    ½-inch slices

1 cup zucchini, sliced into ½-inch
    slices

2 cups *Loma Linda® Vege-Burger®*

¼ teaspoon red pepper flakes

½ teaspoon onion powder

½ teaspoon seasoned salt

1 clove garlic, minced

½ teaspoon salt

2 12-inch round pizza crusts

Place water in a medium-sized skillet. Sauté the onion over medium-high heat. When the onions are almost clear, add the remaining ingredients and simmer until vegetables are done. Spread 4 cups of sauce over each pizza. Bake at 350 degrees for 20 to 25 minutes.

Pizza is a favorite at the Johnson household, and now that I am dean of girls at Great Lake Adventist Academy, I have a whole dorm full of girls that love pizza! Some of the girls do not eat cheese so they are very thankful when I make a vegan option for them. Even the girls that like the cheese pizza enjoy the vegan one. This pizza sauce is also good on French bread, English muffins, and buns. Serve it with your favorite vegetable salad and dessert. —Linda

Yield: 12 slices

*(1 slice) Calories 210 Total Fat 3.5g Saturated Fat 0g Sodium 670mg Total Carbohydrates 35g Fiber 2g Protein 9g

Potluck

Asian Vegetable Noodles

3 8-ounce packages brown rice noodles

1 large onion, diced

1 20-ounce can *Worthington® Vegetable Steaks™*, cut into small pieces, reserve liquid

2½ cups carrots, coarsely diced

2½ cups celery, diced

1½ cups water

1½ tablespoons McKay's Chicken Style Seasoning

2½ cups fresh green beans, cut into thirds

2 cups water chestnuts, sliced or diced

4 tablespoons Bragg Liquid Aminos

1½–2 tablespoons dark sesame oil

Prepare the brown rice noodles according to package directions and set aside. In a large skillet, place the onion, *Worthington® Vegetable Steaks™*, and the liquid from the can. Sauté on medium-low heat until onions are clear and the steak pieces are lightly browned, stirring often to avoid burning.

In another large skillet, place the carrots and celery. Mix the McKay's Chicken Seasoning and the water together, then pour over the carrots and celery. Cook over medium-low heat until carrots are almost tender. Add the green beans and continue to cook until the green beans are tender but still firm.

Remove from heat and pour into a very large mixing bowl. Add the noodles, *Worthington® Vegetable Steaks™* mixture, the water chestnuts, and the Bragg Liquid Aminos. Gently toss to combine all ingredients. Drizzle the dark sesame oil over the top and gently toss again until well mixed. Serve immediately, or place in a casserole dish that has been sprayed with a nonstick cooking spray. Cover with foil and refrigerate until ready to heat. When you are ready to heat, leave covered, then place in a 350-degree oven for approximately 30 minutes, or until hot.

Whenever I take this to a potluck, it is one of the first dishes to be eaten, and someone always asks me for my recipe! Make sure you use the dark sesame oil as it gives it that delicious Asian taste and smell. The brown rice noodles as well as all the vegetables give this dish a lot of flavor, texture, and nutrition. Make this and take it to your next potluck—pretty sure there won't be any left for you to take home!
—Cinda

Yield: 25 1-cup servings

(1 cup) Calories 140 Total Fat 1g Saturated Fat 0g Sodium 370mg Total Carbohydrates 28g Fiber 2g Protein 5g

Bulgarian Goulash

In a large skillet on medium-high heat, place all the ingredients except for the macaroni and cook for approximately 15 to 20 minutes. Add the macaroni and cook for another couple of minutes. Serve hot.

The smell of goulash always brings a warm, cozy feeling to me. Mom made this family favorite at least once a week when we were kids, and we all loved it! I still make goulash, and it has become one of my husband's favorite dishes. Serve this delicious yet simple dish with a fresh vegetable salad, homemade bread, and your favorite dessert.
—Linda

6 cups fresh tomatoes, chopped

1 teaspoon McKay's Beef Style Seasoning

1¼ cups onion, diced

1 teaspoon salt

½ teaspoon seasoned salt

1 teaspoon onion powder

½ teaspoon red pepper flakes

1 cup *Loma Linda® Vege-Burger®*

1 15.5-ounce can kidney beans

1 15.5-ounce can chili beans

4 cups cooked macaroni

Yield: 12 1-cup servings

(1 cup) Calories 180 Total Fat 1.5g Saturated Fat 0g Sodium 760mg Total Carbohydrates 31g Fiber 5g Protein 11g

Stroganoff Casserole

1 20-ounce can *Worthington® Choplets®*, reserve liquid

1 large sweet onion, diced

4 teaspoons VegeSal

6 cups fresh baby portabella mushrooms, coarsely chopped

3 cups original unsweetened almond milk

¾ cup Wondra flour or very finely ground flour

1 teaspoon salt

1 12-ounce container Tofutti Better Than Sour Cream

6 cups farro, cooked according to package directions

Cut each of the *Worthington® Choplets®* into 3 strips, then cut each strip into thin slices. Spray a large skillet generously with nonstick cooking spray; add onion, *Worthington® Choplets®* slices, liquid from the choplets, 1 teaspoon of VegeSal, and the mushrooms. Sauté on medium-low heat until onion is clear and *Worthington® Choplets®* slices are lightly browned. Remove from heat and set aside.

In a medium saucepan, add the almond milk, Wondra flour, salt, and the remaining VegeSal. Mix with a wire whisk until well blended. Bring to a boil over medium heat until thickened, making sure to stir constantly, approximately 2 to 3 minutes. Add the Tofutti Better Than Sour Cream and mix well. Remove from heat and add to the sautéed choplet mixture. Stir to thoroughly combine.

Spray an 11 x 8 x 3-inch casserole dish with nonstick cooking spray. Spread 2 cups of the sauce evenly over the bottom, and then gently spread 3 cups of the cooked farro over the sauce. Spread 3 cups of the sauce over the farro and then add the remaining farro. End with the remaining sauce over the top. Bake in a 350-degree oven for 30 minutes, or until hot and bubbly. Remove from oven and let stand for 5 minutes before serving.

My son David loved my stroganoff casserole when he was in elementary and middle school. Back then I made it with brown rice, and would put it hot in a thermos for him to take to school for his lunch. The farro is a delicious as well as very nutritious substitution for the brown rice. But if you can't find farro in your area, just use the same amount of brown rice. I actually like the short grain brown rice best, but medium or long grain will be good too. —Cinda

Yield: 12 1-cup servings

(1 cup) Calories 260 Total Fat 7g Saturated Fat 0g Sodium 1310mg Total Carbohydrates 45g Fiber 6g Protein 13g

Spinach Manicotti

For Sauce: In a large skillet, sauté the onion in the olive oil on medium-high heat until the onions are clear in color. Add the garlic herb spaghetti sauce, seasonings, and *Loma Linda® Vege-Burger®*. Simmer for approximately 20 to 25 minutes.

For Spinach Filling: Place all the filling ingredients in the blender, except the spinach and Parmesan cheese. Blend until smooth. Pour into a medium-sized bowl and stir in the chopped spinach and ¼ cup Parmesan cheese. Stir until well blended.

Fill each cooked manicotti shell with spinach filling. Spray a 9½ x 13½ x 2-inch glass dish with nonstick cooking spray and pour half of the sauce in the bottom of the dish. Lay the stuffed manicotti shells on top and cover with the remaining sauce. Sprinkle the remaining ¼ cup Parmesan cheese on top and bake at 350 degrees for 30 to 45 minutes. Serve with a vegetable salad, homemade garlic breadsticks, and a favorite dessert.

This is one of those dishes that can be made up the day before and baked the next day, so it makes a great potluck dish to pass around at a church function. I even like to make extra for leftovers. It is one of those dishes that tastes even better the day after it is baked. Hope you enjoy it as much as my family! —Linda

Sauce:

2 cups onions, finely diced

2 tablespoons olive oil

6 cups garlic herb spaghetti sauce

½ teaspoon salt

½ teaspoon seasoned salt

½ teaspoon garlic powder

1 19-ounce can *Loma Linda® Vege-Burger®*

Spinach Filling:

1 12.3-ounce package firm Mori–Nu tofu

1 14-ounce package water-packed tofu

½ cup Grapeseed Vegenaise

¼ cup Tofutti Better Than Sour Cream

2 teaspoons McKay's Chicken Style Seasoning

¼ cup nutritional yeast flakes

½ teaspoon garlic powder

4 cups fresh spinach, steamed and chopped

½ cup vegan Parmesan cheese

16 manicotti shells, cooked according to package directions

Yield: 16 manicotti

(1 manicotti) Calories 220 Total Fat 8g Saturated Fat 1.5g Sodium 770mg Total Carbohydrates 21g Fiber 4g Protein 16g

Tuscan Valley Lasagna

9 cups water

5 tablespoons McKay's Chicken Style Seasoning

3 cups instant polenta

1 medium onion, diced

1 10-ounce box *Gardenburger Veggie Medley®* Veggie Burgers

1 teaspoon VegeSal

1 teaspoon Italian seasoning

8 cups baby portabella mushrooms, sliced

3 cups marinara or spaghetti sauce

6 cups fresh baby spinach leaves, shredded

1 cup fresh basil, chopped

4 cups vegan mozzarella cheese

In a medium-deep kettle, heat the water to a boil. Add the McKay's Chicken Style Seasoning and then slowly and constantly stir in the polenta. Continue to stir until it thickens, approximately 2 to 3 minutes. Pour equally between three 9 x 13-inch glass baking dishes that have been sprayed with nonstick cooking spray. Working quickly, spread the polenta evenly in each pan. Set aside to cool.

Spray a large skillet generously with nonstick cooking spray. Crumble the *Gardenburger Veggie Medley®* Veggie Burgers and sauté them with the onion over medium-high heat until onion is clear and burger is browned. Stir frequently and spray again with the nonstick cooking spray if it begins to stick to the pan. Add the VegeSal and Italian seasoning and stir to mix well. Remove from heat and set aside. Spray another large skillet generously with a nonstick cooking spray and sauté the mushrooms on medium-low heat until mushrooms are tender firm. Remove from heat and set aside.

Cover one of the pans of cooled polenta with 1 cup of marinara or spaghetti sauce. Spread half of the mushrooms on top and then place half of the sautéed burger and onion mixture evenly over the mushrooms. Next, sprinkle half of the shredded baby spinach leaves evenly over the mushrooms, then some of the fresh basil leaves, and then a third of the vegan cheese. Invert one of the polenta layers on top and repeat layers. Invert the third polenta layer on top and spread the rest of the vegan cheese evenly over the polenta. Bake at 350 degrees for approximately 30 to 45 minutes or until hot and bubbly. Remove from oven and let sit for 10 minutes before cutting into squares and serving.

I love polenta and actually prefer this instead of the traditional lasagna noodles. This is also a great recipe for those who cannot have gluten. During the summer when our garden is overflowing with zucchini and summer squash, I sauté them and add to the lasagna. You can also use your favorite mushrooms if you don't have the baby portabellas. I like to have an extra bowl of marinara or spaghetti sauce on the table so each person can spoon some over their piece if they prefer. —Cinda

Yield: 12 squares

(1 square) Calories 440 Total Fat 11g Saturated Fat 3g Sodium 2070mg Total Carbohydrates 71g Fiber 8g Protein 9g

Vegetable Lasagna

Preheat oven to 350 degrees. Spray a large skillet with nonstick cooking spray. Add onions and **Loma Linda**® Tender Bits and sauté over medium heat until onions are clear. Add peppers, then when slightly tender, add remaining vegetables and spices and sauté until vegetables are tender. Remove from heat, pat the vegetables dry, and set aside.

Spray a 9 x 13-inch glass baking dish with nonstick cooking spray, then spread ⅔ cup spaghetti sauce evenly over bottom of dish. Layer with ⅓ of the lasagna noodles, ⅓ of the vegetables, and ⅔ cup sauce. Repeat, layering in the same order, twice more, for a total of three layers, ending with sauce. Place glass dish on a baking sheet and place in oven. Bake for approximately 40 minutes, or until hot and bubbly. Serve hot!

I'm not a huge fan of lasagna, basically because I don't eat cheese that the traditional recipe calls for, and I'm not fond of tofu as a replacement. So, I came up with this recipe and it's one that I can honestly say I love! The red pepper flakes are the "secret ingredient!" You can use your homemade sauce or your favorite purchased sauce. My favorite from the grocery store is Prego Mushroom Sauce. It has just the right balance of savory with a hint of sweetness! —Brenda

1 medium onion, slivered

1 20-ounce can **Loma Linda**® Tender Bits, sliced thin

2 cups red, yellow, or orange sweet peppers, slivered

4 cups fresh mushrooms, sliced

5 cups yellow summer squash, sliced in in ¼-inch rounds, then cut in half

5 cups zucchini, sliced in ¼-inch rounds, then cut in half

1 teaspoon sweet basil

2 teaspoons parsley

1 teaspoon red pepper flakes

2 teaspoons salt

2 cloves garlic, minced

¼ teaspoon oregano

6 cups spaghetti sauce of your choice

1 package no-cook lasagna noodles OR whole grain lasagna noodles, cooked according to package directions

Yield: 12 squares

(1 square) Calories 160 Total Fat 4g Saturated Fat 0.5g Sodium 1170mg Total Carbohydrates 24g Fiber 6g Protein 9g

Taco Lasagna

1 large onion, diced

3 cloves fresh garlic, minced

2 cups orange, red, and yellow mini
   sweet peppers, cut into small
   slivers

1 tablespoon ground cumin

1 tablespoon chili powder

1 tablespoon dried oregano

2 teaspoons paprika

1 teaspoon onion salt

1 teaspoon garlic powder

Salt to taste

1 9.5-ounce package *MorningStar
   Farms* Roasted Garlic and
   Quinoa Burgers, thawed and
   crumbled

1 16-ounce can pinto beans, drained
   and rinsed

1 15.5-ounce can black beans, drained
   and rinsed

1 4-ounce can diced green chilies

1 tablespoon jalapeños, chopped
   (optional)

2 cups frozen corn

36 corn tortillas

4 cups fresh spinach, coarsely
   chopped

6 cups salsa

Spray a large skillet generously with nonstick cooking spray and sauté the onions on medium-low heat until clear. Add the garlic, peppers, spices, and crumbled *MorningStar Farms* Roasted Garlic and Quinoa Burgers and continue to sauté until lightly browned. Add the beans, green chilies, jalapeños, and corn and sauté until hot.

Spray a 9 x 13-inch casserole dish with nonstick cooking spray and layer 12 corn tortillas in the bottom. Spread 2 cups of salsa over the top of the tortillas, and then sprinkle 2 cups of the shredded spinach over the salsa. Place ½ of the taco mixture evenly over the shredded spinach. Begin layering again with 12 more tortillas on top of the taco mixture and repeat the layers. After you have placed the last 12 tortillas over the top, spread the remaining 2 cups of salsa over them. Place in a 375-degree oven for 45 minutes. Remove from oven and let stand for 5 minutes. Then cut into 15 pieces. Serve with more salsa, nondairy sour cream, and slices of avocado.

Brenda's grandsons were over playing at my house when I came up with this recipe, and they both tried it. The first thing Michael said was, "Auntie Ceda—this is cookbook worthy!" Even Jason loved it! Which is something coming from someone who would love to see vegetables outlawed! —Cinda

Yield: 15 pieces

(1 piece) Calories 200 Total Fat 3.5g Saturated Fat 0.5g Sodium 940mg Total Carbohydrates 34g Fiber 8g Protein 9g

Garden Chili Pasta

In a large skillet, on medium-high heat, place the water and onions and cook for approximately 10 minutes. Add the remaining ingredients except for the pasta and cook for 15 to 20 minutes. Serve hot over pasta.

This sauce can be served over any kind of pasta. Add your favorite garden vegetables while it is cooking. It can also be spooned over English muffins or French bread and topped with vegan mozzarella cheese then baked in the oven at 350 degrees for 10 to 15 minutes or until cheese is melted. —Linda

1 cup onions, finely chopped

½ cup water

1 cup sweet yellow pepper, diced

2 cups eggplant, cut into medium-sized pieces

2½ cups broccoli florets

½ teaspoon garlic, minced

1 teaspoon red pepper flakes

1 teaspoon salt

1 teaspoon seasoned salt

3½ cups diced canned tomatoes

3 cups garlic herb spaghetti sauce, or favorite kind

1 20-ounce can *Worthington*® Chili

1 pound angel hair pasta, cooked according to package directions

Yield: 12 1-cup servings

(1 cup) Calories 250 Total Fat 4g Saturated Fat 0.5g Sodium 910mg Total Carbohydrates 45g Fiber 4g Protein 13g

Beef Enchiladas

1 tablespoon olive oil

1 cup onions, finely diced

2 cups potatoes, cooked and diced

½ teaspoon salt

1 teaspoon seasoned salt

1 teaspoon McKay's Chicken Style Seasoning

½ teaspoon red pepper flakes

1 19-ounce can *Loma Linda® Vege-Burger®*

1 cup corn, frozen or fresh

3 cups mild salsa

3 cups petite-diced tomatoes

¼ teaspoon cayenne pepper

16 corn tortillas

In a large skillet on medium-high heat, place the olive oil and onions and sauté the for approximately 5 minutes. Add the potatoes and seasonings. Continuing sautéing until the onions and potatoes are golden in color. Add the *Loma Linda® Vege-Burger®* and corn and sauté for another 10 minutes.

In a medium-sized bowl, mix together the salsa, tomatoes, and cayenne pepper. Spray a 9 x 13 x 2-inch glass dish with nonstick cooking spray. Spread half of the salsa on the bottom of the dish. Spoon a heaping ¼ cup of filling on the edge of each corn tortilla and carefully roll it up. Place the rolled corn tortilla in the baking dish, seam side down. Top with the remaining salsa and garnish with vegan cheese if desired. Bake at 350 degrees for 20 to 25 minutes. Serve hot.

We really enjoy Mexican food! I like to decorate the table the night before with a colorful Mexican blanket and a sombrero in the middle of the table, some candles, and bright colored dishes. It's fun to do little things like this to make my family and friends feel loved. One thing I like about these Beef Enchiladas is that they can be made the night before and baked the next day. Garnish the enchiladas with jalapeño peppers or with vegan tofu cheese, black olives, and avocado slices. Serve it with Tofutti Better Than Sour Cream and salsa.
—Linda

Yield: 16 enchiladas

(1 enchilada) Calories 130 Total Fat 2g Saturated Fat 0g Sodium 580mg Total Carbohydrates 19g Fiber 4g Protein 10g

Cornbread Taco Casserole

Prepare cornbread according to directions or recipe. Spread into a 11 x 7-inch glass casserole dish that has been sprayed with a nonstick cooking spray. Bake at 350 degrees for 15 minutes.

While the cornbread is baking, sauté the onion in the oil over medium heat until almost clear, then add the *Worthington*® Vegetarian Burger, spices, and corn and continue to sauté until corn and *Worthington*® Vegetarian Burger are beginning to brown. Add the black beans and stir to combine. When the cornbread is done baking, remove from oven and spread the *Worthington*® Vegetarian Burger mixture evenly on top.

In a separate bowl, mix the Tofutti Better Than Sour Cream and vegan cheese together and then gently spread on top of the burger. Return to the oven for another 20 to 25 minutes or until heated through. Remove from oven and cut into 18 pieces. Serve warm with diced tomatoes and avocado.

You can also make individual serving sizes by baking them in muffin cups or mini tart pans. Then you can have a variety of toppings and let each person make their own. They are good warm or room temperature, which makes them perfect for a buffet or picnic. —Cinda

1 package or recipe of your favorite cornbread

1 medium onion, diced

1–2 tablespoons oil

1 20-ounce can *Worthington*® Vegetarian Burger

1 teaspoon salt

2 teaspoons chili powder

1 teaspoon ground cumin

½ teaspoon garlic powder

½ teaspoon onion powder

½–1 teaspoon red pepper flakes

¼ teaspoon dried oregano

½ teaspoon paprika

2 cups frozen corn

1 16-ounce can black beans, drained and rinsed

1 cup Tofutti Better Than Sour Cream

1 cup vegan shredded cheddar cheese

Yield: 18 pieces

(1 piece) Calories 260 Total Fat 9g Saturated Fat 1.5g Sodium 610mg Total Carbohydrates 32g Fiber 4g Protein 11g

Beef Burrito Casserole

1 medium onion, diced

1 19-ounce can *Loma Linda® Vege-Burger®*

2 tablespoons taco seasoning

1 cup water

3 15-ounce cans hot chili beans, with sauce

8 whole-wheat tortillas, torn in bite-sized pieces

1 cup taco sauce

½ cup green chilies

¼ cup jalapeño nacho slices

1 cup salsa

1 cup baked tortilla chips, crushed

Spray bottom of a 9 x 13-inch casserole dish with nonstick cooking spray. Set aside. In a large skillet sprayed with a nonstick cooking spray, sauté onion over medium heat until clear. Add *Loma Linda® Vege-Burger®*, taco seasoning, and water. Cook until all liquid is absorbed. Set aside.

Divide remaining ingredients in half, except for the crushed tortilla chips, to make two layers. Layer in the baking dish in the following order: chili beans, torn tortilla pieces, taco sauce, burger mixture, green chilies, jalapeño nacho slices, and salsa. Repeat layers and spread crushed tortilla chips over top. Cover with foil and bake at 375 degrees for 45 minutes. Remove foil and bake for an additional 15 minutes, or until hot and bubbly. Serve with Spanish rice and warm tortillas.

This dish encompasses so many of the familiar flavors that I so enjoy in Mexican food! It is a meal all in itself! Right before serving, I suggesting covering the top with shredded lettuce, and diced tomatoes! Don't forget to have a big bowl of guacamole on the side! —Brenda

Yield: 12 1-cup servings

(1 cup) Calories 260 Total Fat 2.5g Saturated Fat 0g Sodium 1350mg Total Carbohydrates 41g Fiber 8g Protein 19g

Hungry Shepherd's Pie

Spray a skillet with nonstick cooking spray. Sauté onion, garlic, and **Worthington**® Vegetarian Burger over medium high heat until onion is clear. Add salt, cayenne pepper, ketchup, bread crumbs, water, Better Than Bouillon Vegetable Base, thyme, and oregano. Mix thoroughly.

Spray a 9 x 13-inch casserole pan with nonstick cooking spray. Press burger mixture evenly on the bottom. Layer with corn.

Place potatoes in a medium-sized bowl and add margarine, milk, and salt. Mash to desired consistency. Layer potatoes on top of corn, then finish with the topping.

Bake at 375 degrees for 1 hour. After 45 minutes, cover with foil to prevent the bread crumbs from burning.

For Topping: Heat soy margarine in a skillet over low heat. Add crumbled bread, Italian seasoning, and thyme, and sauté until golden brown.

Finding a recipe that appeals to a large number of people can be challenging, but shepherd's pie is definitely the exception to this rule. I think it's because it's a basic down-home recipe that people love! You just can't go wrong with meat and potatoes, and when you add the **Worthington**® Vegetarian Burger, *meat eaters almost think it's the real thing! —Brenda*

1 medium onion, diced

2 cloves garlic, minced

1 20-ounce can **Worthington**® Vegetarian Burger

¼ teaspoon salt

⅛ teaspoon cayenne pepper

1 tablespoon ketchup

1 cup Italian bread crumbs

1½ cups water

1½ teaspoons Better Than Bouillon Vegetable Base

⅛ teaspoon thyme

1 teaspoon oregano

1 15.5-ounce can white corn, drained

8 cups (or 6 medium) potatoes, peeled, diced, and cooked (1 teaspoon salt when cooking)

½ cup original unsweetened almond milk

2 tablespoons soy margarine

Salt to taste

Topping:

3 tablespoons soy margarine

2 cups whole wheat bread, crumbled

½ teaspoon Italian seasoning

⅛ teaspoon thyme

Yield: 12 squares

(1 square) Calories 240 Total Fat 4g Saturated Fat 1g Sodium 860mg Total Carbohydrates 38g Fiber 5g Protein 14g

Italian Meatloaf

1 medium onion, chopped fine

2 cups cooked lentils

1 cup original almond milk

1 19-ounce can *Loma Linda® Redi-Burger*™

3 cups Pepperidge Farm bread crumbs

2 cups quick oats

2 cups walnuts, chopped

2 0.7-ounce packages Good Seasons Italian Dressing mix

1 teaspoon parsley

1 cup cooked brown rice

¼ teaspoon cayenne pepper

2 cups ketchup

Sauté onion over medium-high heat in a skillet that has been sprayed with nonstick cooking spray. Place all ingredients except ketchup in a large mixing bowl and mix thoroughly. Place in a 9 x 13-inch pan that has been sprayed with nonstick cooking spray. Spread evenly to the edges. Cover completely with ketchup. Bake at 375 degrees for one hour.

Being raised a vegetarian, I grew up on many varieties of "Mom's meatloaf," and she taught my sisters and I the basics of what ingredients to put together to get the most nutrition. She also taught us the tricks of what holds it together without using eggs! I'm always creating a new loaf, and this one I liked because of the combination of the **Loma Linda® Redi-Burger**™*, walnuts, and brown rice. The oats and bread crumbs serve as the binders and the Good Seasons Italian Dressing Mix packs in the flavor! My grandson Michael wanted to name it "Five Star Loaf" but he finally accepted my simpler title!*
—*Brenda*

Yield: 24 slices

(1 slice) Calories 200 Total Fat 8g Saturated Fat 1g Sodium 290mg Total Carbohydrates 24g Fiber 4g Protein 10g

Glazed Veggie Meatballs

In a large-sized skillet over medium-high heat, sauté the onions in olive oil with salt, seasoned salt, and Bragg Liquid Aminos until the onions are clear.

In a large bowl, mash the **Loma Linda® Redi-Burger™** and add the sautéed onions, nutritional yeast flakes, and crushed croutons. Mix until well blended. Form into 1-tablespoon-size balls. Spray a cookie sheet with nonstick cooking spray and place the meatballs on the tray. Spray the top of the meatballs with the nonstick cooking spray and bake at 400 degrees for approximately 20 minutes.

Transfer the meatballs to an 8 x 10-inch baking dish and pour the glaze over each meatball. Bake at 400 degrees for approximately 15 minutes. Remove from oven and serve hot.

For Glaze: Combine ingredients in a small saucepan and cook over medium-high heat, stirring often until well blended.

This sauce is quick and easy and only takes about five minutes to make. I like to serve these meatballs with baked or scalloped potatoes, steamed broccoli, fresh vegetable salad, and one of our favorite desserts. You can make and freeze the meatballs ahead of time, so all you need to do is add the sauce before serving. —Linda

2 cups onions, finely diced

2 tablespoons olive oil

½ teaspoon salt

½ teaspoon seasoned salt

2 tablespoons Bragg Liquid Aminos

1 19-ounce can *Loma Linda® Redi-Burger™*

2 tablespoons nutritional yeast flakes (optional)

1½ cups seasoned croutons, crushed

Glaze:

1 cup ketchup

½ cup fruit-sweetened apricot jam

1 tablespoon Bragg Liquid Aminos

Yield: 50 meatballs

(1 meatball) Calories 40 Total Fat 1g Saturated Fat 0g Sodium 160mg Total Carbohydrates 6g Fiber<1g Protein 3g

Pepper Steak

2 medium green tomatoes

1 medium onion, slivered

2 cloves garlic

2 cups red, yellow, and orange sweet
    peppers, slivered

½ teaspoon red pepper flakes

½ teaspoon salt

2 cups fresh mushrooms, sliced

1–2 cups all-purpose flour

2 20-ounce cans *Worthington*®
    Vegetable Steaks™

4 cups whole canned tomatoes, with
    juice

Submerge green tomatoes in hot boiling water for 1 minute to soften. Remove skin and sliver. Spray a skillet with nonstick cooking spray and sauté onion and garlic over medium-high heat until onion is clear. Add peppers, green tomatoes, red pepper flakes, salt, and mushrooms and sauté until tender.

Place **Worthington® Vegetable Steaks™** in a Ziploc bag containing flour. Shake to coat. Remove **Worthington® Vegetable Steaks™** from bag and discard remaining flour. Spray another large skillet with nonstick cooking spray. Sauté steaks over medium high until golden brown on both sides. Place in a 9 x 13-inch pan that has been sprayed with nonstick cooking spray. Top with vegetables. Squeeze whole tomatoes in a bowl, then pour over the top of the vegetables. Bake at 350 degrees for 1 hour.

*Pepper Steak is one of my favorite veggie dishes, and the green tomatoes really make this recipe. That and the **Worthington® Vegetable Steaks™**! I grew up with this meat substitute, and I love the flavor and texture. To me, texture is just as important as the flavor, and unfortunately with many veggie products the texture can be disappointing. This product is versatile too! If I need vegeburger, and I don't have any on hand, I just take these steaks and grind them in the food processer and in an instant, I have vegeburger! Yup! I love **Worthington® Vegetable Steaks™**! —Brenda*

Yield: 12 1-cup servings

(1 cup) Calories 100 Total Fat 1g Saturated Fat 0g Sodium 470mg Total Carbohydrates 10g Fiber 3g Protein 14g

Steak Caponata

Place **Worthington® Vegetable Steaks™** in a Ziploc bag containing flour. Shake to coat. Remove **Worthington® Vegetable Steaks™** from bag and discard remaining flour. Spray a large skillet with nonstick cooking spray. Sauté steaks over medium-high heat until golden brown on both sides.

In a separate large skillet that has been sprayed with nonstick cooking spray, sauté onion over medium heat until clear. Add peppers, mushrooms, garlic, salt, eggplant, and red pepper flakes. Continue to cook until eggplant is brown and a bit wilted. Add tomatoes, sugar, and lemon juice. Turn heat down to low. Add **Worthington® Vegetable Steaks™** and mix well. Serve over brown rice, farro, or whole-wheat pasta.

This is not a very "juicy" sauce, so if you want more sauce, add extra tomatoes, but then you'll probably want a touch more salt.
I personally like it just the way it is over farro! The reason I cut the steaks in half is because that's the way my mom always cut them.
I asked her about why that was, and started laughing when she told me, "I only did that to save money! With five kids it was expensive, so I sliced them to make them stretch a little further." Ha! So, if you want to skip that part you can, but I still like them sliced! —Brenda

1 cup all-purpose flour (more if needed)

1 20-ounce can *Worthington® Vegetable Steaks™*, sliced in half lengthwise and into bite size pieces

1 medium onion, diced

1 medium sweet yellow pepper, coarsely chopped

1 cup fresh mushrooms, sliced

2 cloves garlic, minced fine

½ teaspoon salt

1 medium eggplant, unpeeled, cut into small cubes

1 teaspoon red pepper flakes

2 cups canned petite-diced tomatoes

2 tablespoons sugar

2 tablespoons lemon juice

Yield: 6 1-cup servings

(1 cup) Calories 150 Total Fat 1g Saturated Fat 0g Sodium 640mg Total Carbohydrates 22g Fiber 6g Protein 15g

Choplets and Gravy

2 20-ounce cans *Worthington® Choplets®*

1 medium onion, diced

4 cups fresh mushrooms, sliced

2 tablespoons soy margarine

½ cup Wondra flour

4 cups unsweetened almond milk

2 tablespoons Better Than Bouillon Mushroom Base

1 teaspoon fresh parsley

1 tablespoon Bragg Liquid Aminos

Slice **Worthington® Choplets®** in half lengthwise. Coat with all-purpose flour. Place on a baking sheet that has been sprayed with nonstick cooking spray. Spray tops of **Worthington® Choplets®**. Place in an oven that has been preheated to 400 degrees. After 10 minutes, remove pan, spray **Worthington® Choplets®** with nonstick cooking spray, and flip. Spray tops and return to oven. Bake for 5 more minutes, then remove from oven.

In a skillet that has been sprayed with nonstick cooking spray, sauté onions and mushrooms over medium heat until onions are clear.

Melt soy margarine in a medium-sized saucepan, then add Wondra flour. Mix together with a fork. Add 2 cups milk and whisk until smooth. Continuing heating until hot and bubbly, then add remaining milk and Better Than Bouillon Mushroom Base, parsley, and Bragg Liquid Aminos. Bring to a boil and simmer until thickened. Add sautéed vegetables and mix well.

Spray a 9 x 13-inch pan with nonstick cooking spray. Add baked **Worthington® Choplets®**. Pour gravy over the top. Bake at 350 degrees for one hour.

This is one of my go-to recipes for dinners at home and is definitely worth taking to potlucks. Growing up, Mom made this dish at least every other week, only she used canned mushroom soup. Since that soup is not a vegan product, I came up with my own sauce, which I love just as much or more! I like to serve it over mashed potatoes, but it's also good with baked potatoes or brown rice. —Brenda

Yield: 16 choplets and gravy

(1 choplet and gravy) Calories 70 Total Fat 2g Saturated Fat 0g Sodium 590mg Total Carbohydrates 5g Fiber <1g Protein 10g

German Skillet Casserole

In a large skillet on medium-high heat, place all the ingredients except for the cooked rice. Cook for approximately 20 minutes, then add the cooked rice and sauté for another 10 to 15 minutes or until cabbage and onions are tender. Serve hot.

Cabbage rolls have always been a family favorite! This skillet casserole is a spin off of cabbage rolls without the roll! Serve it with a fresh vegetable salad and a special dessert. —Linda

2 cups hot water

1 cup onions, diced

4 cups cabbage, shredded

4 cups canned whole tomatoes, crushed

2 teaspoons salt

1 tablespoon McKay's Beef Style Seasoning

1 cup *Worthington*® Vegetarian Burger

1 14.4-ounce can sauerkraut, drained

2 cups cooked rice

Yield: 8 1-cup servings

(1 cup) Calories 140 Total Fat 1.5g Saturated Fat 0g Sodium 1360mg Total Carbohydrates 24g Fiber 5g Protein 8g

Vegetable Moussaka

12 cups eggplant, cut into medium-sized cubes

4 cups zucchini, cubed

4 cups yellow squash, cubed

4 cups yellow, orange and red peppers, cut into thin strips

1–2 tablespoons extra virgin olive oil

1 large onion, diced

1 20-ounce can *Worthington® Vegetable Steaks™*, cut into small thin strips

2 cups fresh or canned tomatoes, including their juices

4 cups fresh mushrooms, sliced

1 tablespoon VegeSal

1 tablespoon dried or fresh oregano leaves, crushed

1 teaspoon ground thyme

8 cups cooked potatoes, sliced

Salt to taste

Heat oven to 425 degrees. Spray a large roasting pan generously with nonstick cooking spray. Place the eggplant, zucchini, yellow squash, and peppers in the pan. Spray the vegetables with nonstick cooking spray and sprinkle with salt. Bake at 425 degrees for 30 to 45 minutes, or until tender and lightly browned. Stir frequently during baking to ensure even browning. Remove from oven and set aside.

In a large skillet, add the extra virgin olive oil, onion, and *Worthington® Vegetable Steaks™*, and sauté over medium high heat until onion is clear and steaks are lightly browned. Add the tomatoes, mushrooms, and seasonings, and simmer for 5 minutes. Remove from heat and set aside.

Spray an 11 x 8 x 3-inch casserole dish with a nonstick cooking spray. Cover the bottom with a third of the sliced potatoes. Place half of the roasted vegetables on top of the potatoes, and then top with half of the tomato mixture. Repeat layers, ending with a layer of potatoes. Spray the top of the potatoes with nonstick cooking spray and place in a 400-degree oven for 45 minutes or until hot and bubbly and potatoes are golden brown and slightly crispy. Remove from oven and let stand for 5 to 10 minutes before serving. Cut into 12 squares.

I traveled to Greece with my family and we all fell in love with the delicious food and warm, friendly people. I discovered that there were many different ways to make moussaka, but almost all of them were made with a cream sauce and lots of cheese. So I decided to come up with my own recipe that would be a healthy version of the traditional one. With the blended flavors of all the fresh vegetables and seasonings, you won't miss the traditional cream sauce and cheese. Don't be alarmed at the amounts of vegetables listed, as they cook down when roasted. You can assemble this the day before and refrigerate until ready to bake. —Cinda

Yield: 12 squares

(1 square) Calories 180 Total Fat 2g Saturated Fat 0g Sodium 550mg Total Carbohydrates 32g Fiber 8g Protein 11g

Cowboy Beans

Place the onions and the water in a microwave-safe container. Cover and place in the microwave on high for approximately 5 to 6 minutes or until tender. Place all the ingredients in a large bowl and mix well. Pour into a baking dish and bake for one hour at 350 degrees. Serve hot or cold.

I like to mix up these beans the night before as the flavors have time to blend together. They are a real hit at picnics, barbecues, church potlucks, and, of course—home! —Linda

1½ cups onions, finely chopped

½ cup water

12 cups canned vegetarian baked beans

½ cup ketchup

1 20-ounce can *Worthington®* Big Franks, sliced

¼ cup molasses

¼ cup pure maple syrup

½ teaspoon seasoned salt

1 teaspoon onion powder

Yield: 28 ½-cup servings

(½ cup) Calories 150 Total Fat 1g Saturated Fat 0g Sodium 470mg Total Carbohydrates 30g Fiber 5g Protein 9g

California Potato Salad

6 cups potatoes, cubed and cooked until tender but firm, cooled

2 cups fresh spinach, coarsely chopped

1½ cups mini red, yellow, and orange peppers, cut into small slivers

½ cup black olives, sliced

1 9.5-ounce package *MorningStar Farms® Grillers®* Chik'n Veggie Patties

Dressing:

¼ cup fresh lemon juice

½ cup extra virgin olive oil

¾ teaspoon salt

2 teaspoons Dijon mustard

1 large avocado, halved, peeled, and seeded

1 teaspoon VegeSal

Place first four ingredients in a large mixing bowl and stir gently to mix. Spray a medium skillet generously with nonstick cooking spray and heat the *MorningStar Farms® Grillers®* Chik'n Veggie Patties patties until both sides are browned and slightly crispy. Cool, then cut into small cubes and toss into the mixing bowl with the vegetables. Pour the dressing over the vegetables and gently toss to mix and coat evenly. Serve at room temperature of refrigerate until ready to eat.

For Dressing: Place all ingredients in a medium-sized jar with a tight-fitting lid. Shake until well blended (avocado halves will mix in and turn the dressing a pale green, but there will be some small chunks of avocado in the dressing). Set aside.

This is a refreshing twist on an old favorite at potlucks. My children, David and Catie, have lemon and avocado trees in their backyard, which really comes in handy when I am cooking at their house! There is nothing like fresh produce picked right from the tree. But even fresh produce picked at your favorite grocery store or farm stand is great too! Get creative when you serve this like, spooning it onto lettuce leaves, or you can put it into pocket bread and serve it as a sandwich!
—Cinda

Yield: 18 ½-cup servings

(½ cup) Calories 140 Total Fat 9g Saturated Fat 1g Sodium 420mg Total Carbohydrates 14g Fiber 3g Protein 3g

Resources

WORTHINGTON AND LOMA LINDA

Worthington® and Loma Linda® provide great vegetarian foods for your daily meals or snacks. As the leading brand of vegetarian foods, their products are low in cholesterol and lower in fat, especially saturated fat, when compared to their meat counterparts. Direct from your pantry or right out of the freezer, these delicious, meatless alternatives are perfect for quick and nutritious meals.

Web site: **www.worthingtonfoods.com**

MORNINGSTAR FARMS

MorningStar Farms® is a division of the Kellogg Company that produces vegetarian food. For more than 25 years, the MorningStar Farms® brand has been offering creative meatless solutions that inspire people to eat well. We want to make meatless eating a part of everyone's life. From breakfast to burgers, we offer a variety of delicious products and recipes. And we won't sacrifice flavor or fun. Because when it comes to going meatless, we want the world to know that there are lots of great-tasting ways to create dishes you can feel good about eating and serving.

Web site: **www.morningstarfarms.com**

GARDENBURGER

For over 25 years, we've made Gardenburger® with real vegetables and grains you can see and taste. We aspire to make the best-tasting vegetarian foods, always with real good ingredients. Each variety of our wholesome veggie burgers is made from simple, honest ingredients you can feel good about. Explore every delicious flavor and Eat Positive!®

Web site: **www.gardenburger.com**

BETTER THAN BOUILLON

Superior Touch offers this line of vegetarian and nonvegetarian concentrated paste food base. Their vegetarian options are made primarily from vegetables, which gives them a richer and more natural flavor than ordinary bouillon cubes or granules.

Web site: **www.superiortouch.com**
Phone: 800-334-4468
Address: Superior Quality Foods
2355 E. Francis Street
Ontario, CA 91761

COUNTRY LIFE NATURAL FOODS

Offers a line of natural, whole, and organic foods at reasonable prices. They carry most of the specialty items in this cookbook such as Mori-Nu Tofu, McKay's Chicken and Beef Seasonings, Bragg Liquid Aminos, pure maple syrup, whole grains, nutritional yeast flakes, herbs, spices, and over 1,200 other natural items. They will ship directly to your house via UPS. Ask for their free catalog.

Web site: **www.clnf.org**
Email: mail@clnf.org
Phone: 800-456-7694

FOLLOW YOUR HEART

Located at Canoga Park, California, they offer Grapeseed Vegenaise, original Vegenaise, Reduced Fat Vegenaise, and a variety of other products. In our opinion this is one of the best on the market.

Web site: **www.followyourheart.com**
Email: info@followyourheart.com
Phone: 888-394-3949

TOFUTTI

Offers a variety of nondairy items that are soy based and casein-free, including sour supreme, cream cheese, cheddar cheese, mozzarella cheese, and cheese slices.

Web site: **www.tofutti.com**
Email: info@tofutti.com
Phone: 908-272-2400
Address: Tofutti Brands, Inc.
50 Jackson Drive
Cranford, NJ 07016

MCKAY'S SOUP SEASONINGS

We use their chicken and beef seasonings in many of our recipes. Our mom cooked with them when we were little girls, and we still love their seasoning today! Their beef seasoning has recently changed, and we like it even better than before! We think you will too!

Web site: **www.mckays-seasoning.com**
Email: mckayssoupmix@bex.net
Phone: 419-531-8963
Address: McKay's Soup Seasonings
336 North Westwood Ave.
Toledo, OH 43607

Substitutions

MILK SUBSTITUTES

Silk Original Creamer is a nondairy creamer that contains no cholesterol or saturated fat.

TOFU

Tofu is an excellent source of protein and contains no cholesterol. It also is an inexpensive substitute for meat, fish, poultry, and cheese.

Silken Tofu is a soybean product with a silky smooth texture. It's great for cheesecakes, pies, puddings, and salad dressings.

Water-packed Tofu comes in soft, firm, or extra-firm. It has to be refrigerated and has a shorter expiration date. Water-packed tofu has a firmer, spongier texture, and it is great for things like mock scrambled eggs. It can be crumbled and will hold its shape, so it is very useful in all kinds of recipes. It can be blended until smooth or sliced or baked or boiled—the ideas are endless. It is a wonderful product.

Mori-Nu Tofu does not have to be refrigerated until opened and has a long shelf life. Mori-Nu is great for making entrees, desserts, salads, salad dressings, dips, soups, mock egg salad, and many other dishes.

OTHER PRODUCTS

Tofutti Better Than Sour Cream is our favorite sour cream substitute. It looks and tastes close to dairy sour cream but is milk and butterfat free. It contains no cholesterol. This product can be found nationally in most health food stores and select supermarkets. Substitute this product in any recipe that calls for sour cream.

Tofutti Better Than Cream Cheese is a great substitute for cream cheese. It is milk and butterfat free and contains no cholesterol. It is great for making entrées, desserts, or just used as a spread for bagels.

Reduced Fat Vegenaise, Grapeseed Vegenaise, and Original Vegenaise, by Follow Your Heart, are great mayonnaise replacements. Grapeseed oil is an excellent natural source of vitamin E and essential fatty acids necessary for normal cell metabolism and maintenance. Vegenaise is found only in the refrigerated sections of your grocery stores.

Bragg Liquid Aminos is an unfermented soy sauce replacement. It can be used in entrées, Asian foods, to marinate gravies, and in any recipe that calls for soy sauce.

Nutritional Yeast Flakes is one of the most perfect foods known. It is a powerful health source of B-vitamins, amino acids, proteins, minerals, enzymes, and nucleic acids. This premium yeast is grown on sugar beets, which are known to absorb nutrients from the soil faster than almost any other crop. As a result, this yeast is exceptionally rich in selenium, chromium, potassium, copper, manganese, iron, zinc, and other factors natural to yeast. It is also gluten free. This yeast can be used as a breading, in entrées, or sprinkled on top of foods like popcorn, tofu scrambled eggs, and so forth.

Rumford's Baking Powder is an aluminum-free baking powder.

Soy Margarine may be found in your local grocery store. Find a brand that is vegan, nonhydrogenated and has no trans fats and no cholesterol.

"Farro is the Italian name for emmer wheat, an ancient strain of hard wheat from the Fertile Crescent in western Asia. Often confused with spelt due to their similar taste and texture, farro comes in *perlato* (pearled) and *semi-perlato* (semi-pearled); opt for semi-perlato as it has more of the fiber- and nutrient-rich bran intact (or buy whole farro if you can find it). It comes in three grades: long, medium or cracked. Purchase one of the intact grades of farro (long or medium) and crack it yourself in a coffee grinder or blender for maximum freshness.

"Farro is beloved in Italy—and more recently in North America and other European countries as well—for its roasted, nutty flavor and distinctive chewy texture. Farro's tough husk makes it more difficult to process than other commercially produced grains, but that husk also helps protect the grain's vital nutrients. With a higher fiber and protein content than common wheat, farro is also especially rich in magnesium and B vitamins. As a type of wheat, farro is unsuitable for those with celiac disease, gluten intolerance or a wheat sensitivity or allergy" (Dr. Andrew Weil, MD, "Cooking With Grains," DrWeil.com, accessed January 31, 2014, www.drweil.com/drw/u /ART03183/How-to-Cook-Farro.htm).

Egg Substitute: 1 tablespoon water plus 1 tablespoon of cornstarch can be used as an egg replacer.

Pecan Meal is simply pecans that have been ground into a fine meal. This product can usually be found in your local grocery store or purchased at larger grocery stores. To make your own, just put the pecans in the blender and blend until it is the right consistency. Walnuts can be substituted in any of our recipes that call for pecans.

VegeSal is a seasoned salt that is available in the health food section of most grocery stores.

Measurements and Equivalents

3 teaspoons	=	1 tablespoon
4 tablespoons	=	¼ cup
5 tablespoons + 1 teaspoon	=	⅓ cup
8 tablespoons	=	½ cup
12 tablespoons	=	¾ cup
16 tablespoons	=	1 cup
1 tablespoon	=	½ fluid ounce
1 cup	=	8 fluid ounces
2 cups	=	1 pint
4 cups / 2 pints	=	1 quart
4 quarts	=	1 gallon

WEIGHT

Metric equivalents rounded

¼ ounce	7 grams
½ ounce	14 grams
1 ounce	28 grams
4 ounces	113 grams
8 ounces (½ pound)	227 grams
16 ounces (1 pound)	454 grams
32 ounces (2 pounds)	907 grams
40 ounces (2¼ pounds)	1.13 kilograms

OVEN TEMPERATURE

Celsius equivalents rounded

Fahrenheit	Celsius	Gas setting
275 degrees	135 degrees	Mark 1
300 degrees	150 degrees	Mark 2
325 degrees	165 degrees	Mark 3
350 degrees	180 degrees	Mark 4
375 degrees	190 degrees	Mark 5
400 degrees	205 degrees	Mark 6
425 degrees	220 degrees	Mark 7
450 degrees	235 degrees	Mark 8
475 degrees	245 degrees	Mark 9
Broil		Grill

¼ teaspoon	=	1.25 milliliters
½ teaspoon	=	2.5 milliliters
1 teaspoon	=	5 milliliters
1 tablespoon	=	15 milliliters
¼ cup	=	60 milliliters
⅓ cup	=	80 milliliters
½ cup	=	125 milliliters
1 cup	=	250 milliliters
1 fluid ounce	=	30 milliliters
2 fluid ounces	=	60 milliliters
8 fluid ounces	=	240 milliliters
16 fluid ounces (1 pint)	=	480 milliliters
32 fluid ounces (1 quart)	=	960 milliliters
128 fluid ounces (1 gallon)	=	3.785 liters

PAN MEASUREMENTS

Muffin Pans

mini	30ml or 1½ tablespoon
regular 1	80ml or ⅓ cup
regular 2	125ml or ½ cup

To check your muffin pan's capacity, for a mini muffin pan pour 1½ tablespoons (30ml) water into 1 hole in your pan. If the water comes right to the top (with none left over) it is 1½ tablespoon capacity. Use the same method to measure regular muffin pans.

Index